INSTANT
HISTORY

Portable Press
An imprint of Printers Row Publishing Group
10350 Barnes Canyon Road, Suite 100, San Diego, CA 92121
www.portablepress.com · mail@portablepress.com

Printers Row Publishing Group is a division of Readerlink Distribution Services, LLC.
Portable Press is a registered trademark of Readerlink Distribution Services, LLC.

Correspondence regarding the content of this book should be addressed to Portable Press, Editorial Department, at the above address. Author and illustration inquiries should be addressed to Welbeck Publishing Group, 20–22 Mortimer St, London W1T 3JW.

Portable Press
Publisher: Peter Norton
Associate Publisher: Ana Parker
Publishing/Editorial Team: April Farr, Kelly Larsen, Kathryn C. Dalby
Editorial Team: JoAnn Padgett, Melinda Allman, Traci Douglas
Produced by Welbeck Non-fiction Limited

Library of Congress Control Number: 2019947989

ISBN: 978-1-64517-053-2

Printed in Dubai

23 22 21 20 19 1 2 3 4 5

All illustrations provided by Noun Project with the exception of pg16 Eddo via Wikimedia Commons

INSTANT
HISTORY

KEY THINKERS, THEORIES, DISCOVERIES, AND CONCEPTS EXPLAINED ON A SINGLE PAGE

SANDRA LAWRENCE

PORTABLE PRESS

San Diego, California

CONTENTS

EARLY MODERN PERIOD

LONG 19TH CENTURY 1789–1914

WAR YEARS

COLD WAR TO PRESENT DAY

INTRODUCTION

History never stands alone. It's rarely even a chain of events.
If anything, it is more like a web of causes and effects, often
stretching back centuries to seemingly unconnected matters.
The only way to see the whole picture is to stand back, look at
what happened where—and work out the connections.

The Age of Discovery, for example, is a broad subject that opens this
book, seemingly at random. The desire to explore was the consequence
of many already-simmering human urges. Some merely wanted to know
what—if anything—was on the other side of the known seas, to fill in the
blank spaces in their charts currently inhabited by imaginary monsters.
Perhaps there would be treasure, spices, minerals, foods, or ideas. Europe's
population was growing; extra land would be useful. Many wanted to trade,
some to settle. A few to conquer.

As new lands, nations, and commodities were discovered, an era of
transcontinental trade began, introducing Europe to exotic items from
strange vegetables to gunpowder. The printing press helped spread news
and ideas. The Renaissance saw staggering works of art and magnificent
buildings, constructed with imported materials and funded by new-found
wealth. Powerful private companies plied the seas, trading in luxuries,
commodities—and people. They were helped by scientific advances in
shipbuilding and weaponry, hindered by a growing underbelly of piracy, often
state sponsored. In the race to colonize new-found continents, European
nations fought each other in every way they knew.

Civilizations in the Middle East and Far East had webs of their own: for every
Sistine Chapel there was a Forbidden City. The Aztec Empire flourished for
centuries before the Spanish arrived, but these worlds collided, and new
webs began.

As colonists carved continents between themselves, their religions were
imposed on the conquered peoples. The Catholic Church, especially, grew ever
more powerful. It resisted others, from the Moors of Africa to breakaways
from its own faith, like Henry VIII's Church of England. It mistrusted those it
had forcibly converted, such as the Jewish *conversos*, instigating the Spanish
Inquisition to root out rotten souls from the old world and new. It didn't go
unchallenged; a new interpretation of Christianity was beginning to defy
the established Church. Puritans and other religious separatists joined the
exodus of European explorers, traders and invaders seeking a new life in the

9

American colonies, even as European ambassadors were sent to the great courts of the Mughal and Ottoman empires.

The ambassadors had less success further east. Fundamental misunderstandings between cultures saw trade with self-sufficient China severely limited and nonexistent with Shogun-ruled Japan. Some continents were still easy pickings. Australia, newly "discovered" by Captain Cook, provided an excellent dumping ground for convicted British criminals. Slavery still powered Europe's plantations, bringing the kind of wealth that built palaces, landscaped gardens, and fueled vast industrial cities back home.

Europe's colonies were maturing. Their people began to realize that, rather than being treated equally with the citizens of their ruling nations, they were being used as wealth generators. Inspired by ideas thrown up by the Enlightenment, and encouraged by civil war in England and, later, revolution in France, one by one they began to demand autonomy, starting in what would become the United States of America.

Freedom for some saw a new yearning for freedom for all. Slavery still blighted most of the Americas and elsewhere. The fight for abolition would take generations and, in the United States, a civil war. Without the industrial revolution, the fight would have been even bloodier. Plantation owners were able, at least in part, to replace forced manual work with machinery. In the mills back home, the working classes were able to produce more in the cities and factories than they had ever managed in the rural world. Railroads transported goods across land and steam ships across the seas, returning with exotic goods from around the world, for those that could afford them. Those who could not were increasingly attracted to new philosophies such as those of Karl Marx, advocating a new kind of world order: communism. Half the population—women—began demanding something more fundamental: the right to vote.

Inventions came thick and fast—the motor car, the light bulb, powered flight. All would have a profound effect on the ever-more complicated twentieth-century web. Flight, for example, allowed millions to experience the world and enabled the transportation of goods, people, and news. It also changed the face of warfare, from zeppelins to atom bombs to 9/11. Two world wars managed to encompass countries half a world from their original sources, often compounding new disagreements with old, festering wounds from a century or more before. Returning soldiers brought home Spanish Flu, a pandemic of a voracity not seen since the Black Death, yet hope also arrived in the form of new medications, discoveries, and innovations. Even as the world descended into a second devastating war, records for human achievement were broken at the Olympic Games, to be constantly improved upon through the rest of the century as humans conquered the highest mountains and deepest oceans.

Small webs grew to large ones. The assassination of one figure could topple many, as in the case of Archduke Ferdinand. With Martin Luther King and Malcolm X, it focused the Civil Rights Movement to new purpose, while a by-product of the assassination of John F. Kennedy put a man on the Moon.

This book cannot begin to encompass every event in history. Even with the moments profiled here, a couple of hundred words do not even scratch the surface of extremely complex subjects. All it can hope to do is show, in easily digestible bullet points, a few of the millions of threads that make up the web of the world. Each entry highlights salient points worth following up later, with an eye to seeing the bigger picture. As patterns emerge and connections build, history's causes and effects become clearer. Understanding what brought us Spanish Flu, the Tiananmen Square Massacre, or the Watergate Scandal is at least part way to knowing how to prevent new versions of old evils.

THE AGE OF DISCOVERY

When the ancient network of trading routes from the Far East to Europe was closed by the Ottoman Empire in 1453, European traders needed to find new ways to transport goods.

EARLY MODERN PERIOD

TIMELINE

Mid-1420s to 1460 Henry the Navigator, Prince of Portugal, sponsors expeditions sailing south, then east along the coast of Africa, colonizing as he goes

1487 Pêro da Covilhã treks across land and sea, through Egypt to the Red Sea

1488 Bartolomeu Dias rounds Africa's Cape of Storms and realizes the coast now heads north

1492 Christopher Columbus believes he has reached the East by sailing around the world; in reality he has found the West Indies

1497 Italian John Cabot hits Newfoundland

1499 Italian explorer Amerigo Vespucci explores the north coast of South America

1500 Pedro Álvarez Cabral discovers Brazil

1511 The Portuguese establish a base at Malacca, commanding the straits of the South China Sea

1512 The Spice Islands and Java are reached

1553 The search for the Northeast Passage begins

1557 A trading port is established at Macao

1576 Martin Frobisher, searching for the Northwest Passage, discovers Frobisher Bay

1670 Hudson Bay Trading Company established

TRADED GOODS

WEST TO EAST
Camels
Slaves
Horses
Grapevines
Furs
Honey
Exotic fruit
Glass
Rugs and carpets
Weapons

EAST TO WEST
Silk
Rice
Jewels
Paper
Tea
Porcelain
Spices
Perfume
Gunpowder
Ivory

TERRA INCOGNITA
Whatever else was discovered there were still blank spots on the map

THE BLACK DEATH

In 1348 two ships arrived at Melcombe in Dorset, bringing to Britain a deadly disease that had already ravaged Europe. Within two years, one third of the population of England, Scotland, Wales, and Ireland were dead.

PLAGUE ROUTES

LATE 1330S
Strange deaths in **Kyrgystan, Central Asia**. Deaths make slow but steady progress **along the Silk Road**

1346
Rumors of the disease **reach Europe**

1347
Plague reaches **Sicily and Italy**; **c.100,000 dead** in Florence

1348
In **Paris**, **c.50,000 die**

1348
From England, the **plague continues to Scandinavia**

INFECTION

"Plague" came in **three forms**. Everyone got **fever**, **headaches**, and **general weakness**.

On top of that:

BUBONIC
Buboes (boils) appear under arms and groin

Boils turn black and fetid

PNEUMONIC
Coughing blood

Trouble breathing

Chest pain

SEPTICAEMIC
Stomach pain

Diarrhea

With no cure, victims died so fast there often weren't enough people left in a village to bury the dead. Corpses were thrown into stinking, communal **"plague pits."**

REPUTED TREATMENTS
Figs
Eggs in vinegar
Rhubarb
Muskroot (herb)
Sweet-smelling posies of herbs and flowers

REVOLTING PEASANTS
After the plague, **workers were in short supply** and felt they had more power. When a **poll tax was mooted in 1381**, it fueled a **Peasants' Revolt**.

BLAME GAME
Black rats have been blamed for plague down the centuries, but some experts now believe **human parasites** may have carried the disease.

UNHAPPY RETURNS
Plague occasionally revisited London; the **worst outbreak** was in **1665**. It still strikes occasionally today, often in Africa. Untreated, it can be fatal.

20 MILLION ESTIMATED DEATHS ACROSS EUROPE

THE BATTLE OF AGINCOURT

In August 1415 an English–Welsh army seized the French port of Harfleur. While marching to Calais, however, King Henry V was informed that a massive French army blocked his path.

 DATE OCTOBER 25, 1415

 LOCATION AZINCOURT, NORTHWEST FRANCE

 COMBATANTS ENGLAND AND WALES VS FRANCE

 COMMANDERS KING HENRY V OF ENGLAND; CHARLES D'ALBRET, COMTE DE DREUX

 ESTIMATED SIZE OF ARMIES ENGLISH 5,000–6,000; FRENCH 20,000–30,000

 TERRAIN NARROW AND MUDDY

 RESULT ENGLISH VICTORY; ONE THIRD OF FRENCH NOBILITY KILLED OR CAPTURED

PREBATTLE

The English and Welsh army was **hungry**, **tired**, and **suffering from dysentery**. No one believed they could win. The night before combat, Henry V walked around the camp encouraging his soldiers, an event immortalized by Shakespeare in his famous **"St. Crispin's Day" speech**.

MODERN WEAPONRY

The English–Welsh archers were experts, **especially with the longbow**. The French had longbows as well, but they were too far back to be useful.

In his 1599 play *Henry V*, William Shakespeare **immortalized the English victory**.

THE HEAT OF BATTLE

The French cavalry, many of whom were nobility, charged. The English held their positions, **firing volleys of arrows**.

Wounded horses panicked; thrown riders were unable to right themselves in their heavy plate armor.

A wave of French infantry trampled their own fallen horses and soldiers, then **got stuck in the mud** themselves.

The English started **taking prisoners for ransom**, but another French attack from behind **forced Henry to order their deaths** until he could stabilize the attack. The French considered this unchivalrous.

WEAPONS

FRENCH		ENGLISH–WELSH
• Two-handed swords	• Daggers	• Mainly the longbow, with armor-piercing arrows
• Maces	• Lances	• Hand weapons
	• Clubs	
	• Longbows	

THE RENAISSANCE

Meaning "rebirth," the Renaissance was a huge cultural outpouring of interest in Classical philosophy, scholarship, science, values, and, above all, art.

 DATES ROUGHLY EARLY FOURTEENTH CENTURY TO EARLY SIXTEENTH CENTURY

HUMANISM

Humanism brought a wave of **interest in secular matters**—those emanating from the human spirit—**rather than everything being initiated by the church**.

PHILOSOPHY

Ancient Greek and Roman ideals, flavored with **medieval concepts of chivalry** and new forms of power politics, would lead to the ultimate guide for Renaissance rulers: **Machiavelli**'s *The Prince*.

INVENTION

The printing press **allowed ideas to circulate freely** across the known world, both ancient—as **many classical texts became available for the first time**—and modern, as new ideas went into overdrive.

FINE ART

The Renaissance saw its **most spectacular flourish in art**, mainly centered around Italy and, in particular, **Florence**. Anatomy was depicted in new and daring ways, while the arrival of **perspective brought life to landscapes**.

SCULPTURE

Two sculptures of the boy-warrior **David**, by **Donatello** and **Michelangelo**, Bandinelli's *Hercules and Cacus*, and Michelangelo's *Moses*, *Pietà*, and *Slaves* are considered some of the finest works the world has known.

SCIENCE

Everything in the world was waiting to be discovered, from **astronomy** to **chemistry, physics** to **the human body**.

ARCHITECTURE

The Renaissance saw the **meeting of classical Roman and Greek architectural theories** with later decorative and modern design concepts. To this day **no one knows how Brunelleschi built the dome on Florence's Santa Maria del Fiore cathedral**.

WARFARE

Gunpowder, perfected in China, had reached early modern Europe and, by the **mid-fifteenth century**, **hand guns** were beginning to change the rules of warfare.

HIGH RENAISSANCE

From the 1490s to 1527, three great artists—**Leonardo da Vinci**, **Raphael** and **Michelangelo**—dominated, though dozens of now-household names such as **Botticelli**, **Titian**, **Donatello**, and **Giotto** also proliferated.

NORTHERN RENAISSANCE

The Northern Renaissance **flowered a little later, from the late 1400s**, in the **Netherlands**, **Belgium**, **France** and **England**, bringing artists such as **Bruegel**, **Dürer**, **Holbein**, and **Van Eyck**.

THE AZTEC EMPIRE

*Of the many peoples of medieval Mesoamerica, the Aztec Empire,
famously defeated by the Spanish, still captures the imagination.*

TIMELINE

200 Aztecs arrive in the Valley of Mexico from the north

1325 Tenochtitlán is founded and grows to be a great city of causeways and canals

1428 The Aztec Empire is founded by an alliance between three peoples and the defeat of a fourth

1440–69 The rule of Moctezuma I marks the zenith of the Aztec Empire

1487 The Templo Mayor is dedicated with thousands of human sacrifices

1502 Moctezuma II begins his reign

1517 A comet is believed to be a sign of doom

1519 Hernán Cortés, a Spanish conquistador, has Moctezuma taken prisoner and killed

1521 Cortés defeats the Aztecs

1522 The City of Tenochtitlán is rebuilt as Mexico City

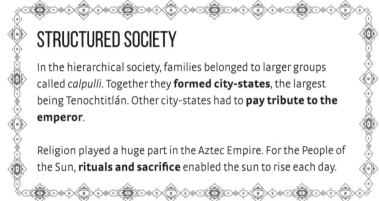

STRUCTURED SOCIETY

In the hierarchical society, families belonged to larger groups called *calpulli*. Together they **formed city-states**, the largest being Tenochtitlán. Other city-states had to **pay tribute to the emperor**.

Religion played a huge part in the Aztec Empire. For the People of the Sun, **rituals and sacrifice** enabled the sun to rise each day.

GODS REVERED AND FEARED

Huitzilopochtli—god of war
Tlaloc—god of rain and water
Quetzalcoatl—god of life and wind
Tezcatlipoca—god of night
Chicomecóatl—goddess of agriculture

AZTEC PYRAMID OF POWER

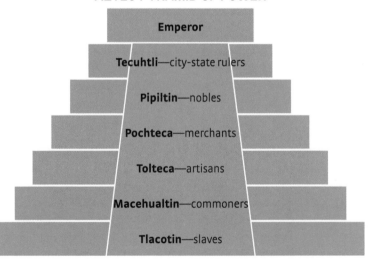

Emperor

Tecuhtli—city-state rulers

Pipiltin—nobles

Pochteca—merchants

Tolteca—artisans

Macehualtin—commoners

Tlacotin—slaves

LEONARDO DA VINCI

The ultimate Renaissance man, Da Vinci was fascinated by everything from science to mathematics, painting to inventing, sculpture to architecture, engineering to caricature.

Everything was a source of wonder to Da Vinci, to be investigated, recorded, and developed. He was just as interested about the **inside of the human body** as the outside, the **possibilities of flying** as much as pushing **concepts of warfare** to their limits.

INVENTIONS

Few of Leonardo's inventions were ever constructed, or would have worked if they had been, but he thought of them first. Among his ideas were **flying machines, tanks, automatic weapons, parachutes, diving gear, self-propelling carts, helicopters**, and even **a robot**.

THE MONA LISA

Painted	1503–19
Hangs	The Louvre, Paris
Medium	Oil on poplar wood
Depicts	Unknown sitter

THE LAST SUPPER

Painted	1495–98
Location	Santa Maria delle Grazie, Milan
Medium	Tempura
Depicts	Christ with the apostles

LOST MASTERWORK

Da Vinci spent vast amounts of time working on a **16 ft., bronze equestrian statue**. The bronze was **eventually used to build cannons instead** and Da Vinci's clay model was lost. Other works were also unfinished during his lifetime.

TIMELINE

- **April 15, 1452** Born in Vinci, Italy
- **c.1467** Trains under artist Andrea del Verrocchio in Florence
- **1472** Accepted in the painters guild but starts making sketches for technical apparatus
- **1482** Moves to Milan to work for the Duke, leaving *Adoration of the Magi* unfinished
- **1502** Begins work for Cesare Borgia as a military architect and engineer
- **1513** Moves to Rome to work for the Pope but receives no major commissions
- **1516** Moves to France as first painter, architect, and engineer to the King
- **May 2, 1519** Dies in Amboise, France

THE PRINTING PRESS

Both printing and presses existed before the fifteenth century, but it took German goldsmith Johannes Gutenberg to mechanize the two.

EARLY MODERN PERIOD

TIMELINE

- **868** *The Diamond Sutra*, the world's oldest complete and dated printed book, is created using seven woodblocks

- **11th century** Bi Sheng, a Chinese artisan, creates moveable type from baked clay

- **c.1400** Johannes Gutenberg is born

- **1439** A lawsuit reveals Gutenberg is working on a printing machine

- **1454–5** The Gutenberg Bible is printed, the first printed book in Europe

- **1473** *The Recuyell of the Historyes of Troye* is the first book printed in English

- **1476** William Caxton sets up a press in London, printing more than 100 books including Chaucer's *Canterbury Tales* and Malory's *Le Morte d'Arthur*

In Europe, before the fifteenth century, **books were laboriously copied by hand**, making them prohibitively expensive.

Xylography (woodblock) printing had been used in **China and Korea for centuries**. It eliminated human copying errors and sped up book creation, but **wore out quickly**.

LINSEED OIL AND SOOT
Key ingredients in Gutenberg's ink recipe

Gutenberg broke down woodblocks to **"moveable type"**—individual, upper-, and lower-case letters and punctuation marks. He adapted designs for the screws used in wine, olive oil, and paper presses, and devised **a moldable metal alloy that did not collapse under pressure**.

THE GUTENBERG BIBLE

48 Number of **known copies** of the Gutenberg Bible

Number of lines in the book's columns, giving it the alternative name **Forty-two-line Bible**

42

The printing press **made book production relatively cheap and fast**, leading to an outpouring of Western literature.

THE SISTINE CHAPEL

The Sistine Chapel ceiling is one of the great works of art and The Creation of Adam *detail is, with Leonardo's* The Last Supper, *one of the most reproduced images in the world.*

 REBUILT BY POPE SIXTUS IV, 1477–80

LOCATION THE APOSTOLIC PALACE, VATICAN CITY

 CEILING COMMISSIONED BY POPE JULIUS II

PAINTED 1508–12

 ARTIST MICHELANGELO BUONARROTI

 DIMENSIONS 132 FT. LONG, 44 FT. WIDE, 68 FT. TALL – THE SAME AS THE TEMPLE OF JERUSALEM DESCRIBED IN THE BIBLE

When he was asked to paint the ceiling, **Michelangelo was working on the Pope's tomb**. He considered himself a sculptor and didn't want the commission, but couldn't refuse it. He returned to paint the altarpiece, *The Last Judgement*, but darkness, strain, and concentration **permanently damaged his eyesight**.

> The **original ceiling** depicted a night sky by **Matteo d'Amelia**

FRESCO

The murals were painted using the **fresco technique**, where pigment is applied to damp plaster.

THE WALLS WERE PAINTED BY ARTISTS INCLUDING:

- Biagio di Antonio
- Sandro Botticelli
- Pietro Perugino
- Domenico Ghirlandaio
- Bartolomeo della Gatta
- Luca Signorelli

THE SISTINE CHAPEL IN NUMBERS

9
Panels at the center, **depicting scenes from Genesis**; the **Pontiff** had **wanted the apostles** but Michelangelo persuaded him

12,000 SQ. FT.
Painted surface area

300+
Figures depicted

25,000
Visitors per day, 5 million per year

1,564
Nudes covered with fig leaves

MARTIN LUTHER

The medieval Catholic Church was richer and more powerful than any monarch.
To many it was also corrupt. For one German monk, enough was enough.

TIMELINE

- **1483** Martin Luther born in Eisleben, Saxony

- **1501** Sent to study law

- **1505** Drops out of school and becomes a monk

- **1507** The price of indulgences (papal pardons) increases sharply

- **1510** Makes a pilgrimage to Rome, where he is shocked at the corruption of the Catholic Church

- **1512** Becomes Dean of the University at Wittenberg

- **October 31, 1517** Presents his *Ninety-Five Theses*; he is accused of heresy

- **1519–20** Continues to attack the church

- **1520** A papal bull threatens Luther with excommunication; he publishes *Against the Execrable Bull of Antichrist* in response

- **1521** Luther translates the New Testament into German, so nonclergy can read it

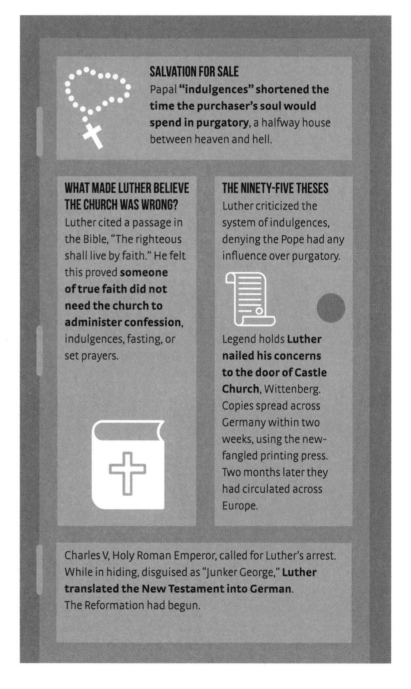

SALVATION FOR SALE
Papal **"indulgences" shortened the time the purchaser's soul would spend in purgatory**, a halfway house between heaven and hell.

WHAT MADE LUTHER BELIEVE THE CHURCH WAS WRONG?
Luther cited a passage in the Bible, "The righteous shall live by faith." He felt this proved **someone of true faith did not need the church to administer confession**, indulgences, fasting, or set prayers.

THE NINETY-FIVE THESES
Luther criticized the system of indulgences, denying the Pope had any influence over purgatory.

Legend holds **Luther nailed his concerns to the door of Castle Church**, Wittenberg. Copies spread across Germany within two weeks, using the new-fangled printing press. Two months later they had circulated across Europe.

Charles V, Holy Roman Emperor, called for Luther's arrest. While in hiding, disguised as "Junker George," **Luther translated the New Testament into German**. The Reformation had begun.

THE BIBLE IN ENGLISH

While it was still in Latin, the Bible was a mystery to most people, and the Catholic Church liked it that way. William Tyndale believed it should be available to everyone.

TIMELINE

- **c.1494** William Tyndale born

- **c.1521** Tyndale ordained as a priest; he moves to London to translate the Bible into English; this was strictly against Church doctrine and he feels threatened

- **1524** Tyndale moves to Germany, seeking the help of Martin Luther, who has translated the Bible into German

- **1525** Tyndale's translation of the New Testament is completed and printed in Cologne; copies are smuggled to England

- **1529** Tyndale is accused of heresy; he goes into hiding

- **1534** Tyndale wrongly believes that King Henry VIII's break with the Pope will make him safer and he moves to Antwerp

- **1536** Tyndale is betrayed, arrested, imprisoned, and executed

- **1539** Henry VIII, having changed his mind, authorizes *The Great Bible*, in English, to be read aloud in church services

- **1557** The Geneva Bible is published; it becomes popular with Puritans

- **1611** The King James version becomes the standard Bible

WHY DID THE CHURCH OBJECT TO AN ENGLISH-LANGUAGE BIBLE?

While only scholars and the clergy could read Latin, **the Church had complete control over their extremely religious society**. If anyone could read the Bible, they would lose power.

EXECUTION

As a heretic, Tyndale was **burned at the stake**. He was allowed to be **strangled first**.

THE GREAT BIBLE

Henry VIII's version used much of Tyndale's work as a base, **changing key passages declared to be objectionable**.

THE KING JAMES BIBLE

The King James Bible, a.k.a. the Authorized Version, is still regarded as one of the **most beautiful works of literature** in the English language. Begun in 1604, it was **translated by forty-seven Church of England scholars**.

NICOLAUS COPERNICUS

Flying in the face of received wisdom, Nicolaus Copernicus suggested that the Earth was not the center of the Universe.

EARLY MODERN PERIOD

TIMELINE

- **February 19, 1473** Copernicus born in Thorn, Poland

- **1491** Enters the Krakow Academy

- **1496** Travels to Italy to study law

- **1503** Returns to Poland and becomes known as an astronomer

- **1508–13** Outlines theories of planetary motion in *Commentariolus*, "Little Commentary"

- **1514** The Pope, looking to modernize the calendar, consults Copernicus

- **1530** His masterwork, *De Revolutionibus Orbium Coelestium Libri VI*, is completed

- **1543** *De Revolutionibus* is published; he dies shortly afterward

- **1616** *De Revolutionibus* is banned by the Catholic Church

Copernicus's **interest in geography and astronomy** began while staying with a **mathematics professor** in Bologna.

Copernicus's theory, often called **"heliocentric,"** proposed that the **planets revolve around a fixed position: the Sun**. He calculated that the Earth took a year to orbit the Sun, rotating on its own axis once a day.

Commentariolus was not published in Copernicus's lifetime but **he gave influential lectures**, which aroused the curiosity of **Pope Clement VII**.

De Revolutionibus Orbium Coelestium Libri VI translates as **"Six Books Concerning the Revolutions of the Heavenly Orbs."**

During his lifetime **Copernicus enjoyed a decent relationship with the Catholic authorities** and their initial reaction to the book was ambivalent. Protestants, including **Martin Luther**, immediately **rejected his theories**.

JOSHUA 10:10–15

The Church's objection was based on a passage in the Bible in which Joshua **bids the Sun and Moon to stand still**.

Copernicus's work was banned after Galileo's trial by the Roman Inquisition. It remained on the list of prohibited books **until 1845**.

THE DEATH OF RICHARD III

Known variously as a Shakespearean villain, the last English monarch to die in battle, and more recently "the King in the car park," Richard III is many things to many people.

TIMELINE

- **1452** Richard, born a younger son of the House of York, is soon to be embroiled in bloody civil war with the House of Lancaster in the Wars of the Roses

- **1461** Richard's brother becomes King Edward IV; Richard himself is made Duke of Gloucester

- **April 1483** Edward unexpectedly dies; Richard is pronounced protector of Edward's twelve-year-old son, Edward V

- **Summer 1483** Richard declares himself king; the uncrowned boy-king and his younger brother disappear

- **August 1485** Henry Tudor, of the House of Lancaster, lands at Milford Haven with an army

- **August 1485** Richard personally leads his troops to meet Henry Tudor at Bosworth, Leicestershire. Leading a charge, he is unhorsed but continues to fight by hand

- Richard is cut down in the melée

- Henry Tudor is crowned Henry VII

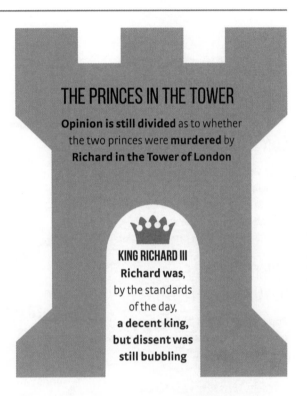

THE PRINCES IN THE TOWER

Opinion is still divided as to whether the two princes were **murdered** by **Richard in the Tower of London**

KING RICHARD III
Richard was, by the standards of the day, **a decent king, but dissent was still bubbling**

Archaeologists discovered a skeleton under a **Leicester car park in 2012**. Radiocarbon dating and DNA proved the body was Richard's and **he was reinterred with honor at Leicester Cathedral in 2015**.

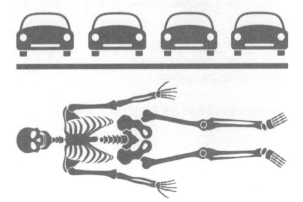

EVIL KING RICHARD

William Shakespeare had every reason to **portray Richard as a villain**—Shakespearean monarch Queen Elizabeth was a descendant of the victorious Henry Tudor.

THE SPANISH INQUISITION

The medieval Catholic Church was deeply suspicious of Jewish people who had converted to Christianity. The methods used to check Christian sincerity were some of the most extreme the world has known.

 DATES 1478–1834

 DEATHS UNKNOWN, SINCE THE PROCESS WAS SECRET; ESTIMATED 30,000–300,000

 LOCATION INITIALLY IN SPAIN, THEN ACROSS EUROPE, NORTH AFRICA, SOUTH AMERICA, AND INDIA

CONVERSOS

After **anti-Semitic pogroms** in **Seville in 1391**, many Jews reluctantly **converted to Christianity**, but were accused of practicing their **own faith in secret**.

EXIGIT SINCERAS DEVOTIONIS AFFECTUS

Pope Sixtus's 1478 papal bull translates as **"sincere devotion required."** Conversos were specifically targeted, but people suspected of **witchcraft, blasphemy, bigamy, Islamism, and Protestantism were also investigated**.

TOMÁS DE TORQUEMADA

(1420–98)

Of all the Dominican friars known as the Hounds of the Lord, **Grand Inquisitor Torquemada was top dog**. He codified the Inquisition's **investigations, interrogation, and punishment**.

TRIAL

After months in prison, conversos were dragged before a secret court

AUTO-DA-FÉ
Ritualized **"Acts of Faith"** where prisoners underwent public penance

28 ARTICLES
Crimes individuals could be accused of under Torquemada. **Anyone could anonymously accuse anyone.**

C.2,000
People burned at the stake under Torquemada

DEATH

Not wanting blood on its hands, the Church handed **"guilty"** individuals to **secular authorities for execution.**

to confess their guilt. **They were not told what they were accused of.**

TORTURE

Officially the "last resort," **torture was not allowed to shed blood.** Methods included:

- Thumbscrews
- Toca (water torture)
- White-hot pincers
- The rack
- *La garrucha* (hanging by the wrists)

Confiscation of property was routine.

Victims wore garments according to their punishment:

SANBENITO

Yellow with a red cross, pointed hat, rope with knots = public flogging
Number of knots in rope = number of lashes received

SAMARRA

Painted with devils; victim surrounded with flame = burning at the stake

FUEGO REVOLTO

Upside-down flames = escaped death through fire

THE FIELD OF THE CLOTH OF GOLD

In June 1520 Henry VIII of England met Francis I of France near Calais. The resulting display of Renaissance opulence became one of the most glamorous parties in history.

 DATE JUNE 7–24, 1520

 LOCATION CALAIS, FRANCE

 HOSTS HENRY VIII OF ENGLAND AND FRANCIS I OF FRANCE

 ATTENDEES 6,000 FRENCH; 6,000 ENGLISH

 THEME GOLD

 DRESS CODE SUMPTUOUS

 AFTERMATH PEACE BETWEEN TWO TRADITIONAL ENEMIES—FOR ABOUT THREE YEARS

BACKGROUND

Charles V of Hapsburg was building an empire, and the Ottomans to the east were bringing pressure on Europe. **England was a small power** in comparison to France, but still a potentially valuable ally. The powerful cleric **Cardinal Wolsey engineered a meeting**.

 ## THE KINGS

Francis and **Henry** had much in common. They were **both in their 20s, tall, handsome, and athletic**, had won battles, loved hunting and the arts, and had an eye for the ladies. **They were curious about each other.**

 ## OPULENCE

Homes, **palaces** and even **Westminster Abbey** were **emptied of plate** and **jewelry**, **tapestries** and **fine Turkish carpets**. People mortgaged their lands to dress in cloth woven with gold. **The sheer amount of wealth on display led to the event's nickname.**

ENTERTAINMENTS

- Jousting
- Feats of arms
- Archery
- Wrestling
- Music
- Feasting

Each event was carefully planned to balance power. The kings wanted to prove they were making peace because they wished to, not because they were weak. On Sunday each king dined with the other's queen.

THE MEETING

The kings rode toward one another as though in war. At the last moment **they turned their horses and embraced.**
40,000 gallons of claret were brought by the English to fill their wine fountain.
The English menu: The fish course included **9,100** plaice, **7,836** whiting, **5,554** sole, **2,800** crayfish, **700** conger eels, **3** porpoises, and **1** dolphin.

ACCOMMODATION

France erected 400 golden tents, decorated with astronomical symbols. **The English built a gigantic, temporary palace** of brick and painted canvas. It had four quadrants, each 300 ft. long, with **classical pillars**, **bay windows**, and **fountains**.

5,000 FT.
Amount of clear glass in Henry's palace

THE MUGHAL EMPIRE

The Mughal rule over most of Northern India and Pakistan saw unprecedented advances in culture, architecture, and, to some extent, religious tolerance.

TIMELINE

- **1526** Babur captures the Turkic Ghur'iat Sultanate of Delhi to control much of Northern India

- **1529** Uttar Pradesh and Bihar are added to the empire

- **1540** Babar's son Humayun briefly loses the empire before his son Akbar reinstates him

- **1605** At Akbar's death, the empire has extended from Afghanistan to the Bay of Bengal, Gujarat to the Deccan region

- **1632** Work begins on the Taj Mahal

- **1707** By the death of Aurangzeb, the empire is at its largest, but dissent is in the air

- **1748** Hindu Marathas overrun northern India after the death of Muhammad Shah

- **1803** Delhi falls under British control

- **1857** Bahadur Shah II, the last Mughal, is exiled for his part in the India Mutiny

THE GREAT EMPERORS

BABUR
1483–1530

Descended from Tamerlane on one side and **Genghis Khan** on the other, Babur seemed destined for leadership. **Under his rule, Hindus are tolerated** and slavery diminishes.

HUMAYUN
1508–56

A **poor emperor**, Humayun was nevertheless a patron and even **practitioner of the arts**.

AKBAR
1542–1605

Muslim himself, Babur's grandson took great **interest in other religions of the world**. He encouraged a culture of literature, art, and music within his court.

JAHANGIR
1569–1627

Although also seemingly **always on campaign**, Jahangir continued the artistic culture of his father's court.

SHAH JAHĀN
1592–1666

A man with a **passion for building**— not least the **Taj Mahal**.

AURANGZEB
1618–1707

A **military man**, Aurangzeb deposed his father and **annexed Vijayapura and Golconda**, but was **religiously intolerant** and did not care for the arts.

FERDINAND MAGELLAN

Portuguese navigator Ferdinand Magellan was the first European commander to cross the Pacific Ocean. He would have also been first to circumnavigate the globe if things had worked out differently.

TIMELINE

- **1480** Ferdinand Magellan born in northern Portugal

- **1511** Is in the fleet that captures Malacca (on the Malay Peninsula)

- **1513** Injures his leg in a skirmish, giving him a permanent limp

- **1517** Falls out with the Portuguese king and travels to Spain to work for King Charles I (later Holy Roman Emperor)

- **1519** Sets sail across the Atlantic

- **1520** Discovers a strait that will allow passage, later named for him

- **1521** Reaches Guam, then the Philippines

- **1521** Killed in a battle between rival chieftains

- **1522** Basque Juan Sebastián del Cano completes the journey back to Spain

THE TREATY OF TORDESILLAS (1494)

The Spanish wanted to prove that the **Indonesian Spice Islands** were in the **WEST**, if one sailed far enough around the globe.

All newly discovered lands belonged to Portugal

Spain had all to the west

370 leagues west of Cape Verde

Magellan believed he would **find a passage** to the **EAST** through **South America**.

Del Cano was allowed to add to his coat of arms *Primus circumdedisti me*—"you were first to circle me."

Spanish sailors were **unhappy at an "enemy" leading the trip**, and **starvation and disease** exacerbated matters. **Mutiny**, when it came, was put down mercilessly by Magellan.

5
ships set sail from Sanlúcar de Barrameda, Spain

3
ships make it through the Magellan Strait

1
ship successfully returns to Spain

THE WIVES OF HENRY VIII

Henry VIII went to extraordinary lengths to provide a male heir to the throne, including passing the Act of Supremacy, pronouncing himself head of the Church of England, dissolving the monastery system, and appointing a new Archbishop of Canterbury who would grant him a divorce.

CATHERINE OF ARAGON

1485–1536

Catherine married Henry's older brother Arthur in 1501 but he died very quickly afterward, so Henry married Catherine himself. She **bore six children**, including three boys, but **only one child, Mary, survived**. In 1527 Henry began proceedings to obtain an **annulment**. They became quite extreme, resulting in the **English King's break from the Pope in Rome**.

ANNE BOLEYN

C.1507–36

In **January 1533 Henry married Anne**, who had refused to become a mere royal mistress.

Anne only produced a surviving **daughter—the future Queen Elizabeth I**. But Henry tired of Anne and on May 19, 1536, she **was executed on a charge of adultery**.

JANE SEYMOUR

1509–37

Henry **married his third wife eleven days after executing his second**. She gave birth to the long-awaited **boy-child, Edward**, on October 12, 1537, but she **died less than two weeks later** from childbed complications.

ANNE OF CLEVES

1515–57

Henry was betrothed to Anne, from Cleves in Germany, without seeing her. When he did meet her in 1540, he wasn't interested. **He married her for political reasons, then divorced her.**

CATHERINE HOWARD

1524–42

Henry married sixteen-year-old Catherine in 1540, but his ardor was dampened when he heard of her premarital affairs. **Court gossip led him to believe she was committing adultery and she was beheaded in 1542.**

CATHERINE PARR

C.1512–48

Henry was fat, old, and ill when he married Catherine Parr in 1543. **She was in love with someone else**, but couldn't refuse the King. She patiently **nursed him until his death in 1547**.

THE REIGN OF QUEEN ELIZABETH I

Henry VIII would have been horrified that his beloved son Edward, bought at such a price, would die young and without issue. He would have been even more disgusted that his second, "illegitimate," daughter would become Queen. Yet Elizabeth, the last Tudor monarch, is still regarded as one of the greatest England has known.

ELIZABETH WAS BORN TO ANNE BOLEYN ON SEPTEMBER 7, 1533, THE WRONG SEX TO KEEP HENRY'S SECOND QUEEN ALIVE MUCH LONGER

DANCE OF DEATH

May 19, 1536
Anne Boleyn
executed

January 28, 1547
Henry VIII
dies

July 6, 1553
Edward VI
dies

November 17, 1558
Mary I
dies

ENGLAND'S GOLDEN AGE

Elizabeth's **reign was relatively peaceful**, allowing time and funds for **world exploration**, **international trade**, **colonial expansion**, and a **renaissance in the arts**.

VIRGINIA

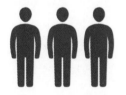

Elizabeth knew she was the **most eligible bachelorette in Europe** and deftly played suitors against one another, both at home and abroad. **She juggled international diplomacy** while firmly remaining the **Virgin Queen**.

RELIGIOUS TOLERANCE—UP TO A POINT

While **adhering to Protestantism**, the Queen had little stomach for persecution. **As long as her Catholic subjects outwardly conformed**, she preferred to ignore what they did in private. Her **spymaster Sir Francis Walsingham**, however, kept a beady **eye out for conspiracy**.

GLORIANA

Elizabeth died in 1603, having ruled for **forty-five years**. Public mourning was unprecedented and genuine.

THE DARK HISTORY OF SUGAR

Most medieval people had decent teeth. The wealthy could afford more honey than the poor, but sugar was an expensive treat. Then Europe found ways of getting its hands on rather more...

EARLY MODERN PERIOD

TIMELINE

- **c.8000 BC** Probable first use of sugar, in New Guinea, gradually spreading through Southeast Asia, China, India, and beyond

- **1096–99** "Sweet salt" is brought back from the Holy Lands by Crusaders as a spice

- **1480** The Portuguese bring sugar to the New World for cultivation

- **1500s** European traders begin shipping enslaved people from western Africa to the Americas to work on plantations for cotton, tobacco, and sugar

- **1600 and 1700s** Sugar prices drop due to slave labor and it becomes the must-have flavoring

- **1747** German chemist Andreas Marggraf discovers sugar in the roots of beet vegetables

A SPOONFUL OF SUGAR

Sugar was originally imported as a **medicine**

WHEN TOOTH-ROT WAS FASHIONABLE

Queen Elizabeth I was so fond of sweet things **her teeth were black**. Her courtiers followed suit, since bad teeth was a sign they could afford sugar. **It was so valuable** it was kept under **lock and key**.

ALT SUGAR

Until **sugar beet** was discovered, the only form of farmable sugar was **labor-intensive cane**.

SUGAR PALACES

Much of Europe's **grandest architecture** was built on **wealth from sugar plantations**.

SUGAR IN NUMBERS

C.70 ships involved in the fifteenth-century Madeira sugar trade alone

C.3,000 sugar mills in the Caribbean and South America in 1550

80%
Amount of European sugar produced in the **West Indies**

20%
Amount of **sugar in all European imports** between 1710 and 1770

MARY, QUEEN OF SCOTS

The story of Mary's romantic, complicated, and ultimately doomed mission to claim her throne is one of the great stories of early modern Europe.

TIMELINE

- **1542** Born at Linlithgow Palace, only child of James V of Scotland; becomes Queen aged six days

- **1547** Betrothed to Prince Edward of England; Mary's guardians object to her marrying a Protestant; Henry VIII tries to abduct Mary in the "Rough Wooing" war

- **1558** Married to Francis, Dauphin of France

- **1559** Becomes Queen Consort of France

- **1560** Francis dies; Mary returns to Scotland

- **1565** Marries her cousin, Lord Darnley

- **1566** Darnley, with several friends, murders Mary's secretary David Rizzio

- **1567** Darnley dies under mysterious circumstances; Mary marries the Earl of Bothwell in apparent unseemly haste and the nobility turn against her; she escapes prison and seeks refuge with her cousin Queen Elizabeth I; she is put under house arrest

- **1586** Tried for treason and condemned to death

- **February 8, 1587** Executed by beheading at Fotheringhay Castle

WHY DID ELIZABETH HAVE MARY ARRESTED?

Elizabeth worried Mary's supporters could **make a claim to the English throne**.

LORD WALSINGHAM

Elizabeth's **spymaster** was on to the continuous conspiracies hatched by Mary's followers. His agents **intercepted, read, then resealed messages**, creating a body of evidence.

THE BABINGTON PLOT

Anthony Babington's plot in 1586, the most serious yet, made Elizabeth realize **Mary was a threat as long as she lived**.

TALK IT OVER

Mary felt if only she could talk with Elizabeth in person, they could work things out, but **the two queens famously never met**.

WHY DIDN'T ELIZABETH EXECUTE MARY SOONER?

Elizabeth felt a **personal connection with Mary** but also feared that **executing a monarch would set a precedent**.

DELAYED VICTORY

Mary's son, **James VI of Scotland**, became **James I of England** upon Elizabeth's death.

56

Number of times David Rizzio was **stabbed**

THE SPANISH ARMADA

*The only major threat to Elizabeth I's largely peaceful reign was quashed
by derring-do and some handy adverse weather.*

 DATES MAY–SEPTEMBER 1588

 LOCATION THE ENGLISH CHANNEL

 COMBATANTS PHILIP II OF SPAIN AND ELIZABETH I OF ENGLAND

 CASUALTIES 20,000 SPANISH KILLED, MANY TAKEN PRISONER; ENGLISH CASUALTIES IN THE LOW HUNDREDS

 RESULT DEFEAT FOR THE SPANISH

TIMELINE

February 8, 1587 Elizabeth executes the Catholic Mary, Queen of Scots; Philip II vows to invade England

April 27–May 1 Sir Francis Drake attacks the Spanish fleet at Cadiz, destroying 100 vessels in a "singeing of the king's beard"

1588 A hastily reconvened Armada of 130 ships sets sail and anchors at Calais

The English attack but are repelled

The English attack with fire ships

The Battle of Gravelines prevents the Spanish landing in England

The Armada is forced to head north, round Scotland and via the west coast of Ireland, where many ships are lost in storms they dub "the Protestant Winds"

1596–97 Two further Armadas are both destroyed by storms

Catholic Spain was Europe's most powerful empire, but Elizabeth I wanted part of the treasure of the New World. **She authorized "privateers" to attack Spanish ships** returning from the Caribbean, and sided with the Dutch bid for freedom from Spanish rule.

BOWLS
Legend tells how **Francis Drake was playing bowls when he heard news of the Armada**, casually finishing his game before attending to the Spanish threat.

BEACONS
A **series of beacons** on hills conveyed the news to Drake, waiting in Plymouth.

THE QUEEN'S SPEECH
On August 8, 1588, Elizabeth addressed her troops at Tilbury, Essex, in a **speech that cemented her popularity**.

THE ARMADA PORTRAIT
To celebrate the victory, **Elizabeth had a new official portrait painted**. It is now on display at the Queen's House in Greenwich.

AFTERMATH
The **defeat of the Spanish Armada** has gone down in the history of England as a victory, but **Elizabeth's power began to decline afterward**, while the Spanish continued to dominate Europe and the New World.

THE WORKS OF WILLIAM SHAKESPEARE

William Shakespeare is hailed as possibly the world's greatest-ever playwright. Written during a golden age of theater, his work stands the test of time, and we often unwittingly quote from him on a daily basis.

 BORN APRIL 26, 1564

 LOCATION STRATFORD UPON AVON, THEN LONDON, ENGLAND

 DIED APRIL 23, 1616

2 EPIC POEMS
The Rape of Lucrece and *Venus and Adonis*

37 PLAYS
can be roughly **divided into three main categories**, though scholars disagree over where some "difficult" plays should be listed.

154 SONNETS
collected and published posthumously in 1609. The **identities of his muses**, the mysterious "Dark Lady" and "Fair Youth," **have never been satisfactorily established**.

11 HISTORY PLAYS
including *Henry IV Parts I & 2*, *Richard II*, and *Henry V*; **most are told from the point of view of the ruling Tudor dynasty**, making rivals, such as in *Richard III*, into villains.

14 COMEDIES
including *Much Ado About Nothing*, *The Comedy of Errors*, *Twelfth Night*, and *A Midsummer Night's Dream*.

12 TRAGEDIES
including *Othello, Macbeth, King Lear*, and *Hamlet*.

THE LAST PLAYS
Some of Shakespeare's final plays are so rich in theme they are difficult to place. For example, *The Winter's Tale* has death but also many comic characters and a theme of redemption.

CONTEMPORARIES
Elizabethan and **Jacobean theater** was full of extraordinary playwrights. **Christopher Marlowe**, **Ben Johnson**, **Thomas Kyd**, **John Webster**, and **Thomas Dekker** all contributed, often in the lurid Jacobean tragedy genre.

THE GUNPOWDER PLOT

*Guards found Guy Fawkes hiding in the shadows with a tinderbox, pocket watch—
and thirty-six barrels of gunpowder.*

 DATE NOVEMBER 5, 1605

 LOCATION THE HOUSES OF PARLIAMENT, LONDON, ENGLAND

EARLY MODERN PERIOD

TIMELINE

1604 Robert Catesby begins recruiting coconspirators

1605 The gang rent space in Parliament's basement and fill it with gunpowder

October 26 An anonymous note reveals the plot to Robert Cecil, the King's spymaster

November 4 Explosives expert Guy Fawkes waits to light the fuse

November 5 Fawkes is arrested

November 8 The rest of the gang are surrounded at Holbeche House; Catesby and Thomas Percy die in a shootout, the others are dragged to the Tower of London

January 1606 All are sentenced to be hanged, drawn, and quartered; Guy Fawkes is lucky—he leaps to his death before being disemboweled

BACKGROUND

James I of England was even more fervent in his **persecution of Roman Catholics** than his predecessor Queen Elizabeth. Robert Catesby's audacious plan would attempt to **extinguish king, court, and government at once**, by **blowing up the Houses of Parliament** as James opened a new session.

TORTURE

Fawkes was tortured, probably on the rack. The signature on his "confession" revealed a broken man.

November 5 is still marked in England with **bonfires** and **fireworks**

The traitors' heads were placed on spikes on London Bridge

THE GOLDEN AGE OF PIRACY

Riches transported between continents in the seventeenth century brought a generation of swashbuckling buccaneers prepared to do anything to steal them.

TIMELINE

1630s Pirates plague the Caribbean, especially the port of Tortuga

1693 Thomas Tew establishes the notorious Pirate Round sailing route

1695 William Kidd is commissioned to hunt down pirates

1701 Captain Kidd hanged for piracy

1706 The Republic of Pirates is established in Nassau

1717 Blackbeard captures a French vessel and renames it *Queen Anne's Revenge*

1718 The Republic of Pirates is reclaimed by the British

1720 "Calico" Jack Rackham hanged for piracy

1721 John Taylor and Olivier Levasseur pull off the biggest single haul of the Pirate Round

1720s The British Royal Navy and commissioned pirate hunters contain the worst of the problem, ending the golden age

PRIVATEERS

In Elizabethan times **"sea dogs"** such as **Sir Walter Raleigh** and **Sir Francis Drake** carried a **"letter of marquee,"** a government **license to attack enemy ships**.

CELEBRITY PIRATES

Back home, a shocked public read dazzling accounts of derring-do, half-idolizing villains such as **Edward "Blackbeard" Teach**, **"Calico" Jack**, **Black Bart**, and **Captain Kidd**.

FEMALE BUCCANEERS

Anne Bonny and **Mary Read** were two of history's most famous pirates. **Grace O'Malley famously met Queen Elizabeth I**, while **Ching Shi** terrorized the South China Sea.

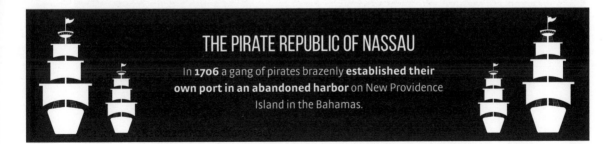

THE PIRATE REPUBLIC OF NASSAU

In **1706** a gang of pirates brazenly **established their own port in an abandoned harbor** on New Providence Island in the Bahamas.

ANA NZINGA

*A highly skilled negotiator, Ana Nzinga, ruler of Ndongo, resisted Portuguese
invasion and fought tirelessly against the international slave trade.*

 DATES C.1581–1661   **LOCATION** THE KINGDOM OF NDONGO, IN MODERN-DAY ANGOLA    **ADVERSARIES** NDONGO VS PORTUGUESE COLONISTS

EARLY MODERN PERIOD

TIMELINE

- **1618** Mbandi deposes his unpopular father, who flees as the kingdom falls into anarchy, but Mbandi also proves cruel and weak

- **1622** Nzinga arrives for peace talks, splendidly dressed. When there is no chair for her, she sits on a servant. She is baptized, taking the Christian name Dona Ana de Souza, to flatter the governor, and negotiates peace. Ndongo is recognized by the Portuguese.

- **1623** Nzinga is made Governor of Luanda

- **1623** The Portuguese renege on their agreement; Mbandi fails to take action, to Nzinga's anger; he dies and Nzinga becomes Queen

- **Nzinga declares Angola a free country**, offering refuge to escaped slaves and **creating the first African–European alliance**, with the Portuguese traders' rivals, **the Dutch**

- **1626 The Portuguese depose Nzinga**; she takes the kingdom of Matamba, **becomes Queen and regroups**; she forms an army and **for three decades personally leads her troops into battle**; she dies Queen of Matamba, at the age of eighty-one

Nzinga's father Kiluanji was an oppressive Ngola (king) who had **made deals with the Portuguese** to allow **limited slave-trading. Nzinga was fiercely against it.**

Both Nzinga and her brother Mbandi were **trained in archery, hunting, diplomacy, and trade**. Nzinga also **learned Portuguese** from a captured missionary.

Nzinga was laid to rest wearing ceremonial leopard skins, with her bow across her shoulder and arrows in her hand

TULIP MANIA

The world's most romantic market crash saw flower bulbs exchange hands for the equivalent of a master craftsman's yearly wage.

📍 **LOCATION** THE NETHERLANDS

TIMELINE

- **Late 1500s** Tulip bulbs start arriving with spice ships

- **1593** Carolus Clusius begins developing glamorous new cultivars in his garden at Leiden

- **Early 1600s** Botanists vie to grow new varieties

- **1636** The boom reaches its peak

- **February 1637** Prices become overinflated; new growers flood the market and the bubble bursts

THE EXOTIC EAST

Tulips came from the Pamir and Tien Shan ranges in Central Asia. The Ottoman Turks were obsessed with growing them and in the late sixteenth century they began to reach Western Europe.

DESIGN CLASSIC

Exotic, flamboyant but in exquisite taste, tulips were everywhere. Specially crafted, **Delftware pyramid vases showed off individual blooms**. Gentlemen posed for paintings clutching them. In England, Inigo Jones included a "tulip" staircase in James I's new palace.

BRING AND BUY

Botanists started to swap them among themselves in taverns and meeting houses. Soon money was changing hands. **Companies were set up to buy and sell to chains of buyers** eagerly awaiting the arrival of a new batch.

THE HEAT IS ON

Prices started to rise. **The best bulbs sold for up to 300 guilders, today about $3,300 (£2,500).** In 1633 it is said properties were being bought using bulbs instead of money, though experts are now divided as to whether regular folk such as carpenters, woodcutters, and bricklayers joined in the speculation.

WHY IS IT SO FAMOUS?

Satirical pamphlets of the time, picked up on by Scottish writer Charles MacKay, deliberately exaggerated the story, and **Tulip traders' "folly" became a good source of hilarity at home and abroad**.

5,000 GUILDERS, 1633

A single *Semper Augustus* bulb

A good-quality house in Amsterdam

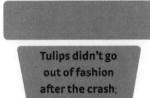

Tulips didn't go out of fashion after the crash; they just reduced to more sensible prices

THE *MAYFLOWER*

In 1620 a ship set sail from England. Among its passengers was a group of religious Separatists, tired of persecution in Europe and seeking a new life in the New World.

 TYPE OF VESSEL CARRACK

 CAPTAIN CHRISTOPHER JONES

 MASTS 3

 DIMENSIONS 90–110 FT. LONG, C.25 FT. WIDE

 ARTILLERY 4 MEDIUM CANNON, 8 SMALL

USUAL CARGO WINE AND DRY GOODS

 SPEED 80 MILES PER DAY

VOYAGE 66 DAYS

WHY DID THE PILGRIMS LEAVE?

The **Protestant Separatists refused to pledge allegiance to the Church of England** and were tired of persecution by the English government.

The **self-styled "Saints" found religious freedom in Holland** but were shocked at the liberal lifestyle there, **so decided to found their own community in America**.

Many passengers were sick and one Stranger was swept overboard.

They landed at Cape Cod on November 9, 1620

THE VOYAGE

In **July 1620** two ships set sail, *Mayflower* and *Speedwell*, but *Speedwell* developed a leak.

On **September 6** and badly delayed, *Mayflower* hit the storm season.

THE MAYFLOWER COMPACT

Forty-one Saints and Strangers signed an agreement establishing themselves as a **legitimate colony**.

ON BOARD

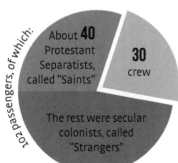

102 passengers, of which:

About **40** Protestant Separatists, called "Saints"

30 crew

The rest were secular colonists, called "Strangers"

53
Number of passengers who survived the first winter

1 MONTH
The duration of the *Mayflower*'s return trip in 1621

C.35 MILLION
Number of American descendants of *Mayflower* passengers

THE EXECUTION OF CHARLES I

Nine years of bloody conflict. Thousands have died but, now the King is captured, what to do with him? Some recommend a quiet poisoning, but the honor of the new regime is at stake…

 DATE JANUARY 30, 1649

 LOCATION BANQUETING HOUSE, LONDON

 AFTERMATH THE COMMONWEALTH RULES UNTIL 1660, WHEN THE MONARCHY IS RESTORED

EARLY MODERN PERIOD

TRIAL

In a packed courtroom, **Charles I wore his hat, a mark of disrespect**. He laughed at the charge of treason, and refused to testify. His belief in the Divine Right of Kings meant he believed only God could overrule his chosen king.

Charles was found guilty. Spared the usual traitor's death—being hanged, drawn, and quartered— **Charles was granted the honor of beheading**.

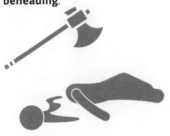

WHY WAS IT IMPORTANT?

Charles's death had implications across the world: **if one monarch could be executed by his own people, so could any other**.

THE EXECUTION

Morning: Charles rises early, dressing carefully for the icy weather. He prays with Bishop Juxon

10:00 a.m.: Charles walks across St. James's Park, surrounded by guards, and into the Banqueting House

2:00 p.m.: Charles is summoned and crosses under Rubens's famous ceiling, stepping through a window, to where the scaffold has been built

The King says a final prayer, removes his cloak and kneels

His head is severed in one blow

The crowd lets out a horrified groan and Charles's head is brandished in silence

WHO KILLED THE KING?

No one knows the executioner's identity. He was heavily disguised and masked.

BLACK SPOT

The clock at Horse Guards still has a black dot marking 2:00 p.m., the King's **hour of death**.

59 "REGICIDES" signed Charles's death warrant; they were later **ruthlessly hunted down**

2 SHIRTS worn by Charles, **in case his shivering from cold made the crowd think he was afraid**

4 HOURS' wait at the Banqueting House, **while the scaffold was made ready**

ELENA CORNARO PISCOPIA

The first woman to receive a PhD proved that universities didn't have to be the domain of men.

TIMELINE

- **June 5, 1646** Piscopia is born in Venice, to the wealthy house of Cornaro

- **Age 7** Takes Greek and Latin lessons

- **Age 11** Takes a secret vow of chastity

- **Age 19** Is regarded the most learned woman in Italy

- **1665** Becomes an oblate (lay-sister who carries out charitable work) after her father refuses to allow her to become a nun

- **1670** Becomes president of the *Accademia dei Pacifici*

- **1672** Studies theology at University of Padua but is refused permission to pursue a doctorate in theology because she is a woman; she is allowed to attempt one in philosophy

- **1677** Debates in front of the entire university, the Senate, citizens of Venice, and foreign visitors

- **1678** Completes her "defense" (oral examination) and achieves her doctorate in philosophy

- **1684** After a lifetime of poor health, religious penances and charitable work, Piscopia dies; memorial services are held in Venice, Siena, Rome, and Padua

7 **The number of languages** apart from one's own needed to earn the title *Oraculum Septilingue*

PISCOPIA EXCELLED IN
Latin
Greek
Hebrew
Spanish
French
Arabic
Chaldaic
Italian

SUBJECTS PISCOPIA STUDIED
Mathematics
Philosophy
Music
Grammar
Dialectics
Astronomy
Theology

INSTRUMENTS PISCOPIA PLAYED
Harpsichord
Violin
Harp
Clavichord
Voice

PUBLIC ORDER

Due to the amount of public interest, **Piscopia's defense** was held in **Padua's cathedral** instead of the university.

AWARDS

On attaining her PhD, Piscopia was presented with:

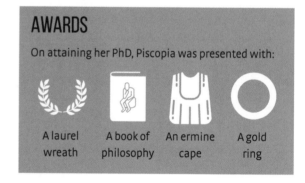

A laurel wreath | A book of philosophy | An ermine cape | A gold ring

AFTERMATH

Piscopia gained **all the credits to be awarded a second PhD in theology** but was **not allowed to receive it**. The University of Padua did **not grant a PhD** to another **woman for more than 300 years.**

THE COURT OF THE SUN KING

The court of King Louis XIV of France was so magnificent he became known as the "Sun King."

LOUIS XIV

 BORN SEPTEMBER 5, 1638

 ASCENDS THRONE 1643

 MARRIES MARIA THERESA OF SPAIN, 1660

 BUILDS HIS PALACE AT VERSAILLES 1661–89

 MOVES INTO VERSAILLES 1682

 DIES SEPTEMBER 1, 1715

When Louis's regent, Cardinal Mazarin, died in 1661, Louis ruled as absolute monarch, **taking the Sun as his badge**. His reign was marked by **almost constant war**, but his court remained resplendent.

VERSAILLES

The **Palace at Versailles**, just outside Paris, was a marvel of **glass**, **gold**, **mirrors**, and **diplomacy**. Every area was carefully arranged and allocated to the "right" people.

GARDENS

Master gardener **Andre Le Notre** laid out his piéce de resistance at Versailles. Some **15,000 acres of lakes, canals, walkways, parterres, and statuary** were surmounted by staggering, pumped fountains, still famous today.

700 rooms at Versailles

4,000+ servants

COURTIERS

All nobles were expected to attend the King. The 5,000-plus courtiers dressed lavishly in the hope of catching Louis's favor. Life was governed by **strict hierarchy and rules of etiquette**.

COURT LIFE

Hunting, balls, romance, music, feasting, business, intrigue, and scandal were a daily part of life at Versailles.

PERSECUTION OF PROTESTANTS

The Edict of Nantes had allowed **Protestants freedom to worship**. After **Louis revoked the Edict**, **200,000 Protestant Huguenots** fled France to **England and Holland**.

ROMANCE

Despite marrying twice, the King also took eleven mistresses and fathered about eighteen children.

THE TAJ MAHAL

Arguably the most beautiful building ever constructed,
the Taj Mahal was built as a love letter to a lost wife.

 MONUMENT THE TAJ MAHAL MAUSOLEUM TO MUMTAZ MAHAL, THIRD AND FAVORED WIFE OF MUGHAL EMPEROR SHAH JAHAN

 LOCATION AGRA, INDIA

 CONSTRUCTED 1632–53

 MATERIAL WHITE MARBLE

 HEIGHT 240 FT.

 ARCHITECT USTAD AHMAD LAHAURI

 NUMBER OF WORKERS 20,000

 NUMBER OF CONSTRUCTION ELEPHANTS 1,000

 COST C.32 MILLION RUPEES (£630 MILLION, OR $830 MILLION, TODAY)

 **Mumtaz Mahal**, "Jewel of the Palace," **died giving birth to her fourteenth child**. Distraught, **Shah Jahan went into mourning**. Poets said his face aged, his back bent, and his hair turned white. He began **to plan a mausoleum** like those of his ancestors, but one that would surpass them all.

MONUMENT OF LOVE

The Taj Mahal's perfect symmetry, exquisite carving, precious stones, and elegant design is in the classical Islamic tradition. It celebrates human love but quotes from the Quran, remembering the spiritual side of life.

PRISONER

In later life **Shah Jahan was imprisoned by his son** Aurangzeb, who declared himself emperor. The aged widower **spent his last days** gazing at his masterpiece from a **window in Agra Fort**.

THE BLACK TAJ

Legend holds Sha Jahan **intended to build a mirror image of his creation in black marble**. There is no evidence this is true.

4,000 SQ. MILES
Protective pollution-free zone
around the monument

7–8 MILLION
Number of
annual
visitors

THE ENGLISH RESTORATION

The resignation of Oliver Cromwell's son, Richard "Tumbledown Dick" Cromwell, paved the way for a return of the English monarchy. With it came a revolution in attitudes, morals, and philosophy.

DATES

 1660 Charles II lands at Dover

 1665 The Great Plague of London

 1666 The Great Fire of London

 1685 Death of Charles II ends the Restoration

Charles II had lost his father's "divine right" and **his actions were largely bound by Parliament**.

WAR

Despite Charles's attempts for peace, Anglo-Dutch wars resurfaced between 1665–67. The navy, having fallen into disrepair, was famously decimated at the Raid on the Medway in 1667. The English had to build a new navy from scratch, ultimately making for a much superior fleet.

SCIENCE

A new wave of **brilliant scientific minds** began working during the Restoration. **Sir Isaac Newton**, **Robert Hooke**, and **Sir Christopher Wren** flourished in true Renaissance style, in disciplines such as astronomy, engineering, and architecture.

COURT ANTICS

After **ten years of sober, Puritan government**, the frothy, gossip-laden court of Charles II heralded a new beginning. **The Merry Monarch** was free-spending (if constantly financially embarrassed) and free-thinking, though **many were shocked at his dissipated lifestyle**.

THEATER

"The play" had been banned under Cromwell. Now it returned with gusto—along with England's first legitimate actresses. One, **Nell Gwyn**, rose from **orange seller to King's mistress**.

SAMUEL PEPYS

Pepys was in the unique position of being a regular citizen who could also move in elevated circles. **His famous diaries lent a wide-ranging and frank perspective to the period.**

68,596 DEATHS
from plague in **1665**

6 VERIFIED DEATHS
in the **Great Fire of London**. In reality there would have been many, many more

30
Charles arrived in London as **King on his 30th birthday**

THE GREAT FIRE OF LONDON

On September 2, 1666, Thomas Farriner's bread oven in Pudding Lane was not put out properly. The City of London would burn for the next five days.

TIMELINE

SEPTEMBER 2

1:00 a.m. The fire starts

7:00 a.m. About 300 houses have burned down

11:00 a.m. Diarist Samuel Pepys arrives at Whitehall to inform King Charles II, who gives the order to pull down houses to create a firebreak

SEPTEMBER 3

9:00 a.m. The Duke of York organizes firefighters

2:00 p.m. The fire destroys the Royal Exchange

SEPTEMBER 4

5:00 a.m. The King brings encouragement to firefighters

12:00 p.m. Ludgate and Newgate prisons are destroyed

8:00 p.m. St. Paul's Cathedral catches fire

10:00 p.m. Enough buildings are torn down to save Whitehall

11:00 p.m. The strong winds reduce, but change direction toward the Tower of London, where gunpowder is kept

SEPTEMBER 5

The fire is eventually extinguished before dawn

Samuel Pepys describes the scene as "the saddest sight of desolation that I ever saw"

THE GREAT FIRE IN NUMBERS

6

Reported deaths, though no one recorded the deaths of poor people, so there would be many more

10,000,000

Estimated cost of the fire, about £1.1 billion ($1.4 billion) today

| **13,200** Homes destroyed | **87** Parish churches razed | **80,000** Homeless |

BLAME

A French watchmaker was tried and executed for setting the fire. He was innocent.

THE GLORIOUS REVOLUTION

The rift between Catholics and Protestants, wrenched apart by Henry VIII, had never fully healed. It opened again in 1688, when the people of England realized they would rather be ruled by a Protestant Dutch prince than a Catholic English king.

THE UNPOPULAR KING

1673 The **Test Acts are passed by Charles II**; all office-holders have to prove they are **not Roman Catholic**

1685 Charles II dies without an heir; his **brother James**, the Catholic Duke of York, is **crowned King**

1686 Misreading the mood of the country, **James repeals the Test Acts;** he fills key positions with Catholics

1687 James's **Declaration of Indulgence suspends all religious penal laws**

THE IMMORTAL SEVEN

A group of peers invited the **Dutch Prince William of Orange**, who was married to Mary, to **invade England**, replacing father with daughter.

15,000
The number of troops accompanying William when he **landed at Torbay in Devon on November 5, 1688**. He was welcomed and, amid anti-Catholic rioting, **many of James's troops switched sides**.

AN INCONVENIENT BABY

In **1688 James had a son**. People who had hoped that, **after James's death**, England would quietly return to his **Protestant daughter, Mary**, saw their dreams shattered.

THE GREAT SEAL

No lawful Parliament could be summoned without the **Great Seal**, so when James fled he flung it **into the Thames**. He spent the rest of his life in exile.

2
Number of crowns needed at the coronation. **William refused to be Mary's consort**, so on **February 13, 1689**, the couple became England's **only-ever joint king and queen**.

THE SALEM WITCH TRIALS

Seventeenth-century New England was obsessed by the belief that witchcraft walked its towns and villages. In Salem "witches" were accused of possessing townsfolk, and hysteria reigned.

 DATE 1692

 LOCATION SALEM, MASSACHUSETTS

TIMELINE

● **January** Betty Parris (nine) and Abigail Williams (eleven) begin having strange "fits" and claiming they've been "pinched"; other young girls begin acting the same way

● **February** The local physician declares them bewitched; accusations begin; three women are identified

● **March–May** Under interrogation, Tituba, the Parris's servant, confesses; the three are sent to prison; more are arrested

● **June** Hangings begin, though Ministers of the Colony warn the court not to rely on "spectral evidence"

● **July** More trials, more convictions, more executions

● **September–October** Confessors begin recanting their testimonies

● **November** A Superior Court of Judicature tries the remaining accused, refusing to use spectral evidence

● **1693** The remaining accused are pardoned

EUROPEAN BEGINNINGS

Witch hunts **began in fourteenth-century Europe**, where an estimated **40,000–60,000 "witches" were executed.**

FAITH

Most people in New England were Puritans—**sober, god-fearing folk with a horror of witchcraft**.

SNOWBALL EFFECT

Accused people were forced to name others, ever-widening the circle. No one was safe but most at risk were unpopular neighbors, single women, "strange" people, and nonregular churchgoers.

SPECTRAL EVIDENCE

Witnesses claimed to have seen a person's specter appear to them, courtesy of the Devil.

WHAT REALLY HAPPENED?

No one really knows. Possible explanations include:

- Asthma
- Lyme disease
- Ergot poisoning
- Epilepsy
- Child abuse
- Delusional psychosis
- Encephalitis

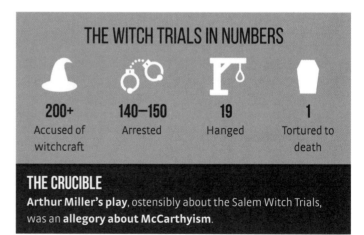

THE WITCH TRIALS IN NUMBERS

200+	**140–150**	**19**	**1**
Accused of witchcraft	Arrested	Hanged	Tortured to death

THE CRUCIBLE
Arthur Miller's play, ostensibly about the Salem Witch Trials, was an **allegory about McCarthyism**.

JOHANN SEBASTIAN BACH

One of the finest composers the world has known, Bach's mastery of musical theory has made him the "musician's musician" for three centuries.

TIMELINE

- **March 31, 1685** Born at Eisenach, Thuringia, Germany

- **1703** Becomes musician at the Weimar court

- **1717** Becomes Kapellmeister (master of music) for Prince Leopold of Anhalt-Köthen

- **1721** Writes the *Brandenburg Concertos* and *The Well-Tempered Clavier*

- **1740** Is losing his eyesight, but continues to work

- **July 28, 1750** Dies

ORGAN TRANSPLANT

Bach was **best known as an organist** during his lifetime. Many of his most famous works are for the instrument, including ***Toccata*** and ***Fugue in D Minor.***

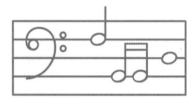

THE WELL-TEMPERED CLAVIER

Bach wrote a series of exercises for students so exquisite that the **forty-eight preludes and fugues** in each of the twelve major and twelve minor keys **are still performed in their own right**.

When **Prince Leopold** offered Bach a job, **his previous employer imprisoned him** in an attempt to get him to stay.

SURGERY

In **1750** Bach bravely tried to restore his failing eyesight by undergoing **risky surgery**. He was left **completely blind**.

COFFEE CULTURE

One of Bach's most **famous operas, *The Coffee Cantata*,** was written to celebrate the **latest fashion in stimulants**.

HIDDEN GENIUS

Little of Bach's work was published before his death, yet he has been **admired by** musicians from **Mozart to Beethoven** ever since.

1,128

Bach compositions survive

THE ENLIGHTENMENT

During the late seventeenth and eighteenth centuries, people began thinking about the world in new ways. The philosophies of the Age of Reason saw science, liberty, and human endeavor begin to eclipse the previously unchallenged "truths" of the Catholic Church and traditional systems of monarchy, paving the way for revolution.

THOMAS HOBBES

1588–1679

In *Leviathan*, Hobbes argued the only civilized way to live is via a **"social contract"** between a ruler and citizens, who **surrender some of their individual liberties** to an absolute sovereign **in return for protection of other rights**.

RENÉ DESCARTES

1596–1650

The French **"Father of Modern Philosophy"** believed in mathematical rigor, scientific observation, and experiment as the way to knowledge, and coined the phrase, **"I think, therefore I am."**

JOHN LOCKE

1632–1704

English philosopher Locke believed **the individual was the result of experience**, and advocated **scientific experiment as a way of gaining truth**.

VOLTAIRE

1694–1778

François-Marie Arouet, writing as "Voltaire," made basic **concepts of freedom**, **religious tolerance, and liberty** accessible to a wider audience.

JEAN-JACQUES ROUSSEAU

1712–78

Geneva-born Rousseau's work, including *A Discourse on the Origin of Inequality* and *The Social Contract*, would fan the flames of the **French Revolution**.

THOMAS JEFFERSON

1743–1826

Jefferson believed **government should protect individuals without breaching citizens' liberty**. He also strove for **separation of religion and the state**.

THE HANOVERIANS

The "Georgian" period was long and, for the most part, prosperous—a time of scientific and artistic enlightenment, when the British Empire began in earnest.

GEORGE I

1714–27

George I, from **Hanover in Germany**, never bothered to learn English. He was **52nd in line to the throne** and unpopular with the public, but he was **Protestant**.

GEORGE II

1727–60

George II had fallen out with his father and **wasn't much liked by the public either**. Several **wars made his reign turbulent**, not least trouble from "Bonnie Prince Charlie," who was still fighting the Jacobite cause.

GEORGE III

1760–1820

George III was the **first of the Hanoverians born in England**. Shy and reserved, he was devoted to his wife, family, and duty. Despite **losing the American colonies** on his watch, and **debilitating mental illness** later in life, he was popular with the public.

GEORGE IV

1810–20

The future George IV was **appointed regent for the last ten years of his father's life**. A dissipated dandy, he was a great lover of the arts, and **the period known as the Regency sparkled with culture**.

1820–30

George IV's public **divorce from his wife, Caroline of Brunswick**, was just one of many reasons the public turned against him, though when **he lost his beloved daughter Charlotte**, the nation rallied.

WILLIAM IV

1830–37

William IV was never intended to reign. He made his life at sea— indeed, he was later known as the "Sailor King"—and came to the throne late in life, aged sixty-four. His reign witnessed several key reforms: an updating of the poor law, the restriction of child labor, the abolition of slavery in most of the British Empire, and perhaps most notably, a wholesale reform of the outdated British electoral system with the passing of the Great Reform Act of 1832.

VICTORIA

1837–1901

One of England's most famous and long-reigning monarchs— her sixty-three years and seven months on the throne was longer than any of her predecessors—Victoria was the last of the Hanoverians. She married Prince Albert of Saxe-Coburg and Gotha in 1840, with whom she had nine children. They married into royalty and nobility throughout the continent, cementing relationships with other European countries, earning her the nickname "the Grandmother of Europe."

THE SOUTH SEA BUBBLE

Lives were ruined and fortunes lost on one of the most frenzied financial speculations in history.

The South Sea Company was formed in **1711** to **trade mainly in slaves**. It assumed that the outcome of the messy ...

↓

War of the Spanish Succession would end with a treaty that would give it a **monopoly of trading in Spanish South America**. Although the resulting ...

↓

1713 Treaty of Utrecht involved punishing **taxes on the slave trade**, and only allowed the company to send **one ship per year**.

↓

Stocks shifted fast, given a juicy, guaranteed interest of 6 percent.

↓

The company's **first voyage was moderately successful**, but when ...

↓

Britain's King George I became governor of the company in **1718**, and investors saw it **paying 100 percent interest**, everyone wanted to buy stocks.

↓

By **1720, Parliament** had allowed the **company to take over the national debt**, and the stock market went crazy. The market couldn't stand the pace. In **August shares started falling**, then tumbling.

↓

By **December, shares had collapsed**, bringing government stock with them.

SOUTH SEA COMPANY STOCKS, 1720

January **£128**
February **£175**
March **£330**
May **£550**
June **£1,050**

August **£800**
September **£175**
December **£124**

AFTERMATH

The House of Commons ordered an inquiry. At least **three ministers had accepted bribes. Robert Walpole came to power**, promising to rout out the culprits. He made an example of some, but let others go.

The **South Sea Company was bought by the Spanish government** and survived until 1853.

LUCKY FOR SOME

Not everyone was ruined. Those canny enough to sell at the bubble's peak became extremely rich.

Satirist **Jonathan Swift**, author of *Gulliver's Travels*, lost money in the collapse, **berating himself in verse**.

THE BATTLE OF CULLODEN

Bonnie Prince Charlie's bid for the Scottish throne was short, bloody, and ultimately defeated, but his role in the Jacobite Rebellion remains a pivotal moment in Scottish history.

 DATE APRIL 16, 1746

 LOCATION DRUMOSSIE MOOR, CULLODEN, SCOTLAND

 COMBATANTS CHARLES EDWARD STUART VS WILLIAM, DUKE OF CUMBERLAND, REPRESENTING THE BRITISH GOVERNMENT

 ESTIMATED CASUALTIES JACOBITES: 1,500–2,000; BRITISH GOVERNMENT: 50

 RESULT THE STUART CLAIM TO THE THRONE WAS QUASHED

THE YOUNG PRETENDER

Charismatic **Prince Charles Edward Stuart**, grandson of James II of England and son of James "The Old Pretender," **was brought up in Rome**, convinced the **thrones of Scotland and England were rightfully his**.

In **1745 24-year-old Charles landed in Scotland**. Ignoring advice to wage guerrilla warfare, he **persuaded powerful clans to join him on a new campaign**, known as **the Forty-five**.

He was **convinced his army would be supplemented**, especially from France.

The **Duke of Cumberland** was recalled from Europe to put **down the rebellion**.

THE BATTLE

Charles's Jacobites faced into **torrential rain and sleet**, hampered by **marshy ground**.

The Scots, fighting with claymores, a variant of the two-handed sword, **were outnumbered, out-maneuvered, and out-equipped** by the British Redcoats' bayonets and muskets.

The **last pitched battle** fought on British soil **was a rout**.

Charles escaped, disguised as **young Flora MacDonald's maid;** his dream of kingship was destroyed forever. Despite a massive reward, **he was betrayed by no one**.

THE DECLARATION OF INDEPENDENCE

One of the most important documents in the history of the United States, the Declaration of Independence pronounced liberty for the colonies, but also proposed that all men are created equal, with unalienable rights.

  DATE JULY 4, 1776

LOCATION PENNSYLVANIA STATE HOUSE, INDEPENDENCE HALL, PHILADELPHIA

 AUTHORS ROGER SHERMAN, BENJAMIN FRANKLIN, THOMAS JEFFERSON, JOHN ADAMS, ROBERT LIVINGSTON

The Declaration was signed by
delegates from all thirteen colonies:

Connecticut
Delaware
Georgia
Maryland
Massachusetts Bay (including Maine)
New Hampshire
New Jersey
New York
North Carolina
Pennsylvania
Rhode Island and Providence Plantation
South Carolina
Virginia

WHAT DOES IT ACTUALLY SAY?

The document states that America's thirteen colonies must be **absolved from all allegiance to the British Crown** and all political connection, and the State of Great Britain totally dissolved. It also lists **twenty-seven grievances against the British Crown**.

EQUALITY FOR ALL?

Native Americans are described as **"merciless Indian savages."** People also continued to **keep African American slaves**.

1,320 WORDS

200
Estimated number of **first-run copies** of the Declaration

26
Known **surviving copies** of the first run

1
Copies signed by all signatories. It's kept in the National Archives at Washington, DC

1 MILLION+
People who see the document each year surrounded by fireworks

4

Independence was declared on July 2, 1776, but the Declaration wasn't formally ratified by Congress until **July 4**. The Declaration **may have been signed later**. The first Independence Day celebration took place the following year. Thirteen gunshots were fired to mark each participating liberated colony.

THE GRAND TOUR

*An eighteenth-century English gentleman's education was not considered complete
until he had taken the Grand Tour of the cultural sites of Europe.*

The tour would start with a rough passage across the English Channel.

In Paris he would admire the art in the **Louvre and Tuileries**, visit **Notre Dame Cathedral** and perhaps treat himself to a **French-made periwig**.

A detour to the **Palace of Versailles** to marvel at the elegance and grandeur of the French Court was de rigeur.

Further south he would sketch the many Roman ruins.

Crossing the Alps was a dangerous business, but the great **sights of Italy** made the dangers worthwhile. The **ancient architecture of Rome** and the newly discovered **Pompeii** and Herculaneum were particular draws and, if he couldn't afford to buy original works of ancient Roman art, there were plenty of copies for sale.

The **social scene in Naples** made the city an essential stop, **not least for the ladies** of all stations he might meet there.

Meeting women was a big consideration traveling north to **Venice**, though the **parties here were legendary**, too. He might even see some art.

According to his budget, a Grand Tourist might choose to also visit **Germany**, **Greece**, **Switzerland**, and **the Low Countries**.

LEGACY

Many stately homes in Britain owe their **neo-classical architecture and stylish contents to the Grand Tour**, as classically trained young gentlemen were inspired by their travels.

THE EAST INDIA COMPANY

Much more than a simple business concern, the East India Company monopolized trade between the British colonies for more than 200 years. It dominated domestic and international politics, furthered imperial expansion, and wielded phenomenal power.

TIMELINE

1600 Elizabeth I grants a Royal Charter to the Governor and Company of Merchants of London Trading into the East Indies

1601 Five company vessels leave for the Spice Islands

1708 The company expands to become the United Company of Merchants of England Trading to the East Indies

1758 Robert Clive becomes Governor of Bengal

1765 Large tracts of India are now governed by the company, which imposes heavy taxes

1773 The company's tea is thrown overboard at the Boston Tea Party

1784 The India Act takes government control of commercial and political interests, weakening the company's power

1857 The India Mutiny further diminishes the company

1858 The British government shifts Indian rule to the Crown

1873 The company ceases to exist

The **world's first limited liability corporation** was formed by a group of **London businessmen** banding together to **share the cost of international trade**.

TRADING IN:
- Silk
- Indigo
- Cotton
- Saltpeter
- Spices
- Tea
- Porcelain
- Opium (illegal)

SLAVERY

From the 1620s the East India Company **used slave labor** and started transporting them, too, reaching a **zenith between the 1730s and 1770s**.

MILITARY INTERESTS

The company maintained **warships and a sizeable standing army of 260,000 men in 1803**. It was also able to call on British naval power and Crown troops.

OPIUM WARS

The East India Company wanted to **trade with China**, buying **tea** and selling **opium** banned by the Chinese government. The company **took an active military role in the Opium Wars** (1839–42 and 1856–60).

WHAT HAPPENED?

Parliament, seeking to curb the company's power, gradually **chipped away at its dominance**, especially in **India**, until it was no longer viable.

THE BRITISH INDUSTRIAL REVOLUTION

Just as science and philosophy enjoyed rapid progress in the eighteenth century, innovations in engineering and applied science amassed their own head of steam.

TIMELINE

- **1709** Abraham Darby smelts iron with coke, a form of processed coal

- **1712** Thomas Newcomen invents the first useful steam engine

- **1771** Richard Arkwright opens the first recognizable "manufactory" at Cromford, near Derby, using his new water frame spinning machine

- **1778** James Watt improves the steam engine

- **1779** The first iron bridge proves what can be done with the material

- **1783–4** Henry Cort introduces puddling and rolling, removing impurities from iron

- **1784** Edmund Cartwright begins work on his power loom

- **1801** Richard Trevithick builds the first moving steam engine

Traditional **cottage industries used one or two workers** in their own homes. **Factories employed hundreds** of people.

Individual tasks became mechanized; laborers would work on one specific part of the manufacturing process instead of making an item from start to finish.

Working conditions in factories and mines were often appalling; child labor was common.

Coal-fueled steam provided constant **reliable power** for newly invented machinery, allowing mass production. **Canals**, **railroads**, and **road-building** improved **communications** and **delivery methods**.

Agricultural mechanization and **enclosure of the countryside** meant less work for rural people. **Thousands moved to new cities** to seek work in the factories.

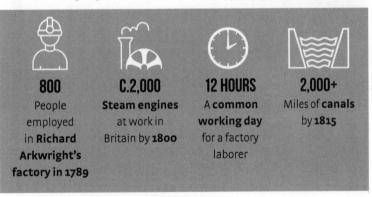

800	C.2,000	12 HOURS	2,000+
People employed in **Richard Arkwright's factory in 1789**	**Steam engines** at work in Britain by **1800**	A **common working day** for a factory laborer	Miles of **canals** by **1815**

TYPICAL JOURNEY FROM LONDON TO MANCHESTER

1700 | 1 | 2 | 3 | 4 | **DAYS**

1870 | 1 | 2 | **DAYS** |

THE ENGLISH LANDSCAPE GARDEN

Wealthy aristocrats returning from the Grand Tour commissioned beautiful new Palladian-style houses to remind them of their travels. Lancelot Brown could see the "capabilities" of their estates to provide the perfect setting.

Wealthy patrons wanted grounds that were **both classical and "British,"** believing previous gardens too geometrical or fussy.

PIONEERS

William Kent (1685–1748) and **Charles Bridgeman (1690–1738)** sowed the seeds in the 1720s and 1730s, marrying the ideas of **grottos**, **temples**, and **Palladian-style bridges** with the natural, **English countryside.**

TIMELINE

- **1716** Lancelot Brown born in Northumberland

- **1724** William Kent begins a new garden at Chiswick House

- **1738** The garden at Stowe House in Buckinghamshire is begun

- **1763** Brown begins work at Blenheim Palace

- **1764** Brown becomes royal gardener

- **1783** Brown dies in London

STOWE

One of the **most influential gardens in the country, Stowe**, was designed by William Kent and Charles Bridgeman. Brown was a gardener there.

Lancelot "Capability" Brown developed the idea into a style that looked effortlessly natural. Brown's look involved **sweeping vistas**, **local landmarks**, and **"eye-catchers,"** including:

- Lakes
- Temples
- Obelisks
- Fancy bridges
- Triumphal columns
- Canals
- Classical mausoleums
- "Oriental" bridges and tea houses
- Lawns
- Ornamental "woods"

He would **flood villages**, **clear woodlands** to one or two artistic clumps, and **move inconvenient hills** to somewhere more picturesque. **Cattle were kept in check** with "ha-ha" sunken walls and **laborers were moved out of sight entirely**.

REPTON

The last of the great landscape gardeners, **Humphry Repton (1752–1818)**, wrote the famous **"Red Books,"** which cleverly showed before and after images of how a gentleman's estate might look if Repton secured the commission.

260

Capability Brown landscapes include:

Petworth, West Sussex
Chatsworth, Derbyshire
Blenheim Palace, Oxfordshire
Clumber Park, Nottinghamshire

400+

Commissions undertaken by **Humphry Repton**

£21,000

Blenheim's landscaping costs (today $5.2 million, £4 million)

A landscape garden was punishingly expensive. Having one showed a gentleman was refined, elegant, politically astute—and wealthy. The craze changed the look of the English landscape forever.

THE HIGHLAND CLEARANCES

The forced eviction of families from large tracts of the Highlands and Western Isles of Scotland caused the breakdown of a traditional way of living—and huge resentment.

 DATES C.1750–C.1880

 WHO PROSPEROUS LANDOWNERS, CLEARING THEIR NEWLY ACQUIRED LAND FOR SHEEP OR CATTLE FARMING, EVICTING THOUSANDS OF TENANTS AND BURNING THEIR COTTAGES

 RESULT MASS EXODUS TO THE INDUSTRIALIZED CITIES; MANY THOUSANDS EMIGRATE TO AMERICA; THE HIGHLANDS BECOME ONE OF THE MOST SPARSELY POPULATED AREAS IN EUROPE

THE CLAN SYSTEM

Before the Clearances **most people lived in "bailes,"** collective groups of smallholdings within clans and under **local chiefs**.

CROFTERS

Some **evacuees were resettled on marginal land**. Economists such as Adam Smith said hardship and necessity would force them to find new ways of subsisting. Some did, fishing and harvesting kelp.

The Crofters Holdings Act 1886 gave some security of tenure to crofters and established a court to rule in disputes between tenants and landlords.

AFTERMATH

By the end of the nineteenth century **even the sheep were largely gone** from the Highlands. By that time, though, many Highlanders and Islanders had made new homes around the world.

BRITISH FEAR

The **clans made the British government nervous**. After the Battle of Culloden, **tartans and bagpipes were banned**. Wealthy, often absentee, landlords were encouraged to begin using their land for "other things" such as sheep farming, and broke up villages as they went.

NUMBERS . . .

. . . are highly contested. Estimates suggest:

C.150,000 **people were evicted** from their homes during the Clearances

C.70,000 **Highlanders and Islanders emigrated** between 1760 and 1800; perhaps as many again in the following sixty years

15,000 people were **evicted from land owned by the Countess of Sutherland and Marquess of Stafford** between 1811 and 1821

WOLFGANG AMADEUS MOZART

The sublime, unique music of Wolfgang Amadeus Mozart sits among the world's great cultural treasures.

TIMELINE

- **1756** Born in Salzburg, Austria

- **1768** Writes his first mass, *Misa Brevis in G*

- **1770** Writes his first opera, *Mitridate Re di Ponto*, at fourteen years old

- **1782** Marries Constanze Weber; they have six children but only two survive infancy

- **1784** Joins the Freemasons; this influences compositions including *The Magic Flute*

- **1787** Gives lessons to sixteen-year-old Beethoven

- **1791** Dies of kidney failure and is buried in a common grave

CHILD PRODIGY

Young Wolfgang could **pick out chords at three years old**, **play short pieces at four**, and **compose by five**. Just before his sixth birthday he and his sister Maria Anna (Nannerl) were taken to Munich, then **Vienna**, where they **played at the Imperial Court**. Life became a whirl of European touring.

MISERÉRE

Gregorio Allegri's masterpiece was jealously guarded and had **never been performed outside the Vatican**. **Mozart heard the work** performed in the Sistine Chapel, then **wrote the entire score from memory**.

MUSIC FAN

Even geniuses need inspiration. Mozart particularly **admired Bach, Handel, and Haydn**.

BEST LOVED WORKS INCLUDE

- *The Marriage of Figaro*
- *Don Giovanni*
- *Cosi fan tutte*
- *Mass in C Minor*
- *Requiem in D Minor*

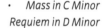

600+ COMPOSITIONS BY MOZART

- **12** violin concertos
- **15** masses
- **17** piano sonatas
- **21** stage and opera works
- **25** piano concertos
- **26** string quartets
- **27** concert arias
- **50+** symphonies

THE BOSTON TEA PARTY

The British Tea Tax, declaring tea could only be imported to America from Britain, created a monopoly for the East India Company. It was the latest of many regulations imposed on the colony by a government the people had no part in.

 DATE DECEMBER 16, 1773

 LOCATION BOSTON, MASSACHUSETTS

 ANTAGONISTS THE BRITISH GOVERNMENT VS AMERICAN COLONISTS

 RALLYING CRY NO TAXATION WITHOUT REPRESENTATION!

 CASUALTIES JOHN CRANE, HIT BY A FALLING TEA CHEST, IS INJURED BUT NOT KILLED

 RESULT NEW RESTRICTIONS CALLED THE COERCIVE ACTS WERE PASSED; THE COLONISTS HAD ANOTHER WORD FOR THEM: INTOLERABLE

SAMUEL ADAMS

Adams had fought many injustices, including the **Sugar Act**, **the Stamp Act**, and the **Townshend Acts**. He made powerful speeches that incensed the public.

LOYAL SONS OF LIBERTY

A **secret society** organized resistance against the British, often rallying underneath the **Liberty Tree**.

THE BOSTON TEA PARTY IN NUMBERS

In fall 1773 **seven British ships leave Britain . . .**

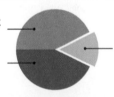

3 dock at Boston
3 turn back

1 is stranded at sea

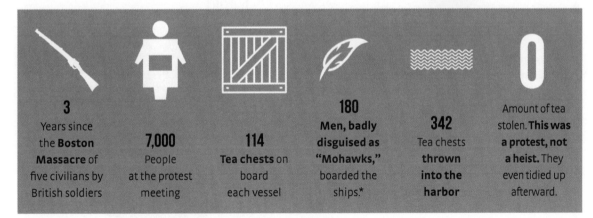

3 Years since the **Boston Massacre** of five civilians by British soldiers

7,000 People at the protest meeting

114 **Tea chests** on board each vessel

180 **Men, badly disguised as "Mohawks,"** boarded the ships.*

342 Tea chests **thrown into the harbor**

0 Amount of tea stolen. **This was a protest, not a heist.** They even tidied up afterward.

* No one knows the real number of "partygoers"—many took their secret to the grave

THE AMERICAN REVOLUTIONARY WAR

The American Revolution saw thirteen North American colonies gain independence from Britain and form into the first United States.

TIMELINE

1756–63 The Seven Years' War proves expensive for Britain. It decides to make the colonies pay toward their own defense

1764 The Sugar Act is the first of a series of deeply unpopular taxes imposed on the American colonies

April 19, 1775 At Lexington, a British army of 700 routs seventy-seven locals. Up to 400 Americans fight back at Concord after being warned by Paul Revere (1735–1818)

June 17, 1775 The Americans are defeated at the Battle of Bunker Hill but inflict serious British losses, boosting their confidence

July 3, 1775 George Washington takes command of the American troops at Cambridge, Massachusetts; he forces the British to evacuate Boston by sea, but fails to invade Canada

July 4, 1776 The Declaration of Independence is made by the thirteen colonies

September 5, 1781 Admiral de Grasse of the French navy enters Chesapeake Bay; Washington brings troops down by land to corner the British

September 28–October 19, 1781 The British are forced to surrender after the Siege of Yorktown

September 3, 1783 The Treaty of Paris sees Great Britain formally recognize the sovereignty of the United States

BACKGROUND

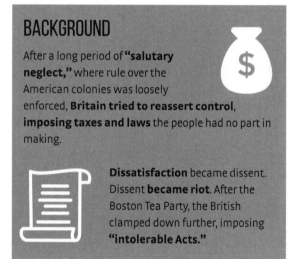

After a long period of **"salutary neglect,"** where rule over the American colonies was loosely enforced, **Britain tried to reassert control**, **imposing taxes and laws** the people had no part in making.

Dissatisfaction became dissent. Dissent **became riot.** After the Boston Tea Party, the British clamped down further, imposing **"intolerable Acts."**

AMERICAN FORCES
(fighting mainly as small, field armies)

231,771
Continental (national) Army

164,087
militias

BRITISH ARMY

42,000
soldiers

30,000
mercenaries
(disciplined professionals)

1/3 colonists loyal to the British

2/3 revolutionaries

THE VOYAGES OF CAPTAIN COOK

Captain James Cook's first mission to the Antipodes sounded peaceful enough: to observe the Transit of Venus. However, he also carried a sealed envelope containing a second goal.

CAPTAIN JAMES COOK

(1728–79)

A **former merchant seaman**, Cook swiftly rose through the ranks of the Royal Navy, making a name for himself as a **captain** and **cartographer**.

THE TRANSIT OF VENUS

Astronomer Royal Edmund Halley (1656–1742) believed Earth's distance from the Sun could be calculated if enough observations were made when **Venus passed in front of the star**.

TERRA AUSTRALIS INCOGNITA

Cook would also, secretly, be searching for a rumored **"Great Southern Continent."**

FIRST VOYAGE

(1768–71)

 Stated mission Observing the transit of Venus

 Sponsors The Royal Society and the British Admiralty

 Ship *Endeavour*, a former merchant vessel

 Official Artist Joseph Banks

 Results Observation of the transit of Venus, charting of New Zealand, claiming Australia's eastern coast for Britain, naming it New South Wales; Cook's men also shoot dead some native New Zealanders

SECOND VOYAGE

(1772–75)

 Mission Search for the Great Southern Continent

 Sponsor The British Admiralty

 Ships *Resolution* and *Adventure*

 Official Artist William Hodges

 Results Crossing the Antarctic Circle three times, making two circuits of the South Pacific, charting islands and island groups unknown by Europeans

THIRD VOYAGE

(1776–79)

 Stated mission To return a Polynesian islander who had come to Britain

 Secret goal Search for the Northwest Passage from the North Pacific to the North Atlantic

 Sponsor The British Admiralty

 Ships *Resolution* and *Discovery*

 Official Artist John Webber

 Results In Hawaii, then unknown to Europe, violence erupts between islanders and the crew; James Cook, four marines and sixteen Hawaiians are killed

 Cook's voyages had a profound influence on the way Europe saw the world, and inspired many more expeditions. Effects on the people he encountered may have been less positive.

GEORGE WASHINGTON

The first President of the United States is still seen as one of America's true patriots.

TIMELINE

- **February 22, 1732** Born in Virginia

- **1752** Joins the colonial militia

- **1756–63** Gains a reputation for bravery during the Seven Years' War (French and Indian War)

- **1759** Marries Martha Custis, joins Virginia House of Burgesses, opposes unfair British taxes

- **1774–75** Attends First and Second Continental Congresses as an outspoken supporter of colonial cause

- **1775** Appointed commander of colonial forces

- **1777** Victory at Saratoga

- **1783** Peace treaty signed with the British

- **1787** Elected president of the Constitutional Convention

- **1789** Becomes the first President of the United States

- **1792** Reelected President

- **1797** Retires

- **December 14, 1799** Dies

POLITICAL FACTIONS

Washington was unhappy that, almost **immediately after independence**, the American government **broke into political parties**: the **Federalists** and the **Democratic Republicans**.

SLAVERY

Washington was **strongly against slavery**. He masterminded the **Slave Trade Act of 1794**, restricting American ships from the slave trade, but when he died, there were **300 enslaved people working on his property**. He decreed they were to be freed on his death. **His wife freed them, and her own slaves, in 1800.**

MOUNT VERNON

Washington **worked his 8,000-acre estate**, rotating crops, fertilizing soil, managing livestock, and taking a **keen interest in the latest scientific innovations**.

THE WHITE HOUSE

The **Residence Act** made the **area of the Potomac River** (later Washington, DC) the permanent **capital of the Unites States**. Washington oversaw the building of the White House but **never lived in it himself**.

THE FIRST FLEET

What do you do when your prisons are overflowing but the criminals keep on coming?
Why not send them to that newly discovered continent on the other side of the world?

 NUMBER OF SHIPS 11

 LEAVES PORTSMOUTH ON MAY 13, 1787

 ARRIVES AT SYDNEY COVE ON JANUARY 26, 1788

 FIRST GOVERNOR CAPTAIN ARTHUR PHILLIP

 NATIONALITIES MAINLY BRITISH CONVICTS BUT ALSO AFRICAN, AMERICAN, AND FRENCH

PEOPLE ON BOARD 1,420

Just 1,373 arrived, due to deaths at sea

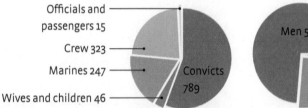

Officials and passengers 15
Crew 323
Marines 247
Wives and children 46
Convicts 789

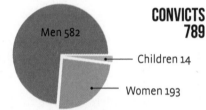

CONVICTS 789

Men 582
Children 14
Women 193

WAS THE FIRST FLEET THE FIRST TO TRANSPORT CONVICTS?

Britain had traditionally sent convicts to America. With the American Revolution they started sending them to **Australia**.

TERRA INCOGNITA

Australia had only been **claimed for Great Britain** by Captain James Cook in **1770**. The land—and its half-million indignant, indigenous inhabitants—was still largely unknown.

CONVICTS' CRIMES

INCLUDED:

- Petty theft
- Burglary
- Highway robbery
- Stealing clothing
- Stealing animals
- Military offenses
- Prostitution
- Fraud
- Political protest

Captain Phillip, having forgotten many practical items, sent for supplies on arrival and **put the prisoners to work**. Among their many skills he found **brickmakers, carpenters, nurses, shepherds, cooks, carters, bookkeepers,** and **administrators**.

The **first convict** to seek a **land grant** was **James Ruse**, a burglar who proved he could farm.

FIRST FLEETERS

By 1792 convicts were beginning to earn their freedom. Some returned to Britain; others decided to take their chances in the New World. **Their proud descendants call themselves First Fleeters.**

THE FRENCH REVOLUTION

In 1789, France—wracked by poverty and famine—was looking for someone to blame. The high-spending clergy and royal family were top of the list. When an unfair land tax was proposed, a revolutionary touch-paper was lit.

TIMELINE

May 1789 King Louis XVI summons the Estates General to vote on his new land tax; the Third Estate convenes a National Assembly under the "Tennis Court Oath"

July 14 The Bastille Prison is stormed; the nobility flee

June 1791 The royal family are captured trying to escape

1792 Abolition of the monarchy

1793–4 The Reign of Terror

July 27, 1794 Robespierre executed

May 18, 1804 Napoleon Bonaparte crowns himself emperor of France

NAPOLEON BONAPARTE
His soldiers discovered the Rosetta Stone in 1799.

THE REIGN OF TERROR

During "the Terror" harsh measures were taken against suspected **"enemies of the revolution."** "Madame Guillotine," originally adopted as a humane method of execution, was kept busy.

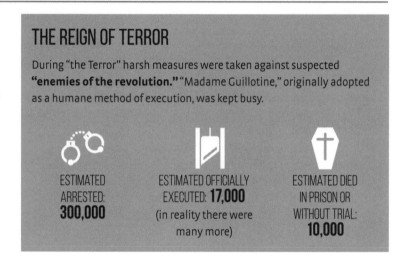

ESTIMATED ARRESTED: **300,000**

ESTIMATED OFFICIALLY EXECUTED: **17,000** (in reality there were many more)

ESTIMATED DIED IN PRISON OR WITHOUT TRIAL: **10,000**

ROLL CALL OF HEADS

LOUIS XVI King of France; he was executed by guillotine

GEORGES DANTON Revolutionary; shocked at the Terror, he **died on the guillotine**

MAXIMILIEN ROBESPIERRE One of the revolution's most **fanatical leaders, he was publicly executed**

JEAN-PAUL MARAT Leader of the radical **Montagnard faction**; assassinated in his bath

THE ESTATES OF THE REALM

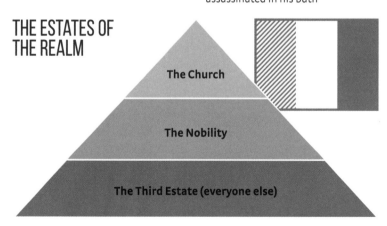

The Church

The Nobility

The Third Estate (everyone else)

BENJAMIN FRANKLIN

Statesman, newspaper editor, diplomat, writer, scientist, and inventor, Benjamin Franklin was a true Renaissance man—and one of the greatest of America's founding fathers.

TIMELINE

- **January 17, 1706** Born in Boston; his father is too poor to send him to school for long, so he is apprenticed to his printer brother

- **1724** Travels to London

- **1726** Resettles in Philadelphia, running the *Pennsylvania Gazette*

- **1748** Now wealthy enough to retire, he concentrates on inventing and science

- **1751** Franklin's scientific papers published as *Experiments and Observations on Electricity*

- **1736–51** Clerk of the Pennsylvania Assembly

- **1750–64** Member of the Pennsylvania Assembly

- **1757–74** In London, he acts as colonial representative of Pennsylvania, Georgia, New Jersey, and Massachusetts

INSTITUTIONS

FRANKLIN HELPED ESTABLISH:

- The American Philosophical Society
- The Library Company
- An academy (later the University of Pennsylvania)
- A firefighting company
- An insurance company
- A hospital

AMONG FRANKLIN'S MANY INVENTIONS:

- The Franklin stove
- Lightning rod
- Battery
- Bifocal glasses
- Odometer
- The glass harmonica
- Daylight saving time
- Rocking chair
- American penny
- The "long arm" for reaching books from a shelf

He also **charted the Gulf Stream** and the distinction between **electrical insulators and conductors**.

FRANKLIN'S KITE EXPERIMENT

Flying a kite during a thunderstorm, Franklin **proved lightning is electricity**.

- **1753–74** As Deputy Postmaster for the Colonies he reorganizes the Post Office; throws himself into the American struggle for independence

- **1776** Helps draft and signs the Declaration of Independence

- **1776** With two others, represents America in France, negotiating the Franco-American Alliance

- **1783** As American Ambassador to France, signs the Treaty of Paris

- **1785** Returns to America to help draft the Constitution

- **1789** President of the Society for Promoting the Abolition of Slavery

- **April 17, 1790** Dies in Philadelphia

EARLY MODERN PERIOD

THE EXECUTION OF MARIE ANTOINETTE

*As she mounted the scaffold, the former Queen of France accidentally trod
on her executioner's foot. Her apology formed her last words.*

LONG 19TH CENTURY 1789–1914

TIMELINE

- **November 2, 1755** Maria Antonia von Hapsburg-Lothringen, fifteenth child of Holy Roman Emperor Francis I, is born

- **April 19, 1770** Marries Prince Louis-Auguste, heir to the throne of France, aged fourteen

- **May 10, 1774** Louis XV dies, Louis XVI is crowned; Marie Antoinette becomes Queen, aged eighteen

- **1778** The arrival of a long-awaited child, the first of four

- **1785–6** A fraud scandal tarnishes Marie Antoinette's name

- **1789** The start of the French Revolution

- **June 20, 1791** The royal family try to flee; they are apprehended at Varennes

- **August 10, 1792** The mob storms the Tuileries Palace; the royal family is imprisoned

- **January 21, 1793** Louis XVI executed

- **October 16, 1793** Marie Antoinette executed

Although popular at first, **Marie Antoinette** enjoyed an **extravagant lifestyle** at court, watched with growing resentment by the **starving lower classes**. She became a **symbol of everything rotten about society**.

THE AFFAIR OF THE DIAMOND NECKLACE

The fraudster in a **high-level jewelry heist implicated the Queen**. She was entirely **innocent** but the mob didn't believe it.

THE REVOLUTION

While the Bastille was being stormed, the royal couple were **mourning their youngest daughter**. Soon after, they also **lost their son** and heir.

EXECUTION

Marie Antoinette, once the **most fashionable woman in France**, was transported to the guillotine in a rough cart. As the executioner brandished her severed head to the crowd, they shouted, ***"Vive la République!"***

NAPOLEON BONAPARTE

One of the greatest military leaders the world has known, Napoleon Bonaparte and the battle tactics he employed are still studied today.

TIMELINE

- **August 15, 1769** Born in Corsica

- **1785** Graduates from the military academy, Paris, 42nd out of 58

- **1789** Fights on the side of the Revolution

- **1796** Bonaparte's military tactics bring victories in Italy

- **1796** Marries Joséphine de Beauharnais

- **1798** Napoleon's army invades Egypt at the Battle of the Pyramids

- **1798** Defeated by Nelson at the Battle of the Nile

- **1799** Takes Paris in a bloodless coup, becoming First Consul

- **1802** The Treaty of Amiens creates uneasy peace with the British

WIVES

Napoleon's famously stormy, fourteen-year relationship with Joséphine ended in 1809, when she did not provide him with a son. He married a reluctant Marie Louise of Austria in 1810.

THE BATTLE OF THE THREE EMPERORS

Napoleon positioned 68,000 troops at the Austrian town of Austerlitz, to look vulnerable. The Russian Czar and Austrian Holy Roman Emperor attacked; Napoleon cut their defenses, killing, wounding, or capturing 26,000 and seeding the dissolution of the Holy Roman Empire.

Number of soldiers guarding prisoner Napoleon on the island of St. Helena:

125 by day

72 by night

- **1804** The Napoleonic Code updates the law of the land

- **1804** Napoleon crowns himself emperor

- **1805** Defeated at the Battle of Trafalgar

- **1805** Napoleon's greatest victory, at the Battle of Austerlitz

- **1812** A bloody, failed campaign in Russia sows the seeds of defeat

- **1814** Forced to abdicate; goes into exile on the island of Elba

- **1815** Retakes Paris and begins a short second rule

- **1815** Napoleon defeated at the Battle of Waterloo

- **May 5, 1821** Dies in exile on St. Helena

BATTLES FOUGHT BY NAPOLEON

lost 7

won 53

29 French soldiers lost at the **Battle of the Pyramids**—the enemy lost thousands

2,281 Articles in the **Napoleonic Code**

84 DAYS Length of Napoleon's "100-day reign"

THE BATTLE OF TRAFALGAR

One of the most mythologized battles in history, Trafalgar cemented supremacy over the waves for Great Britain, at the cost of its greatest-ever naval commander.

 DATE OCTOBER 21, 1805

 LOCATION CAPE TRAFALGAR, SOUTHWEST SPAIN

 COMBATANTS BRITAIN VS FRANCE

 COMMANDERS ADMIRAL LORD NELSON VS VICE-ADMIRAL PIERRE-CHARLES VILLENEUVE

 CASUALTIES 1,700 BRITISH KILLED OR WOUNDED; 6,000 FRENCH CASUALTIES; NEARLY 20,000 FRENCH PRISONERS

 RESULT BRITISH VICTORY

LEAD-UP

After the **Treaty of Amiens broke down in 1803**, both sides waited for the other to move. In **1804, Spain joined with France**. Nelson chased one Franco-Spanish fleet to the West Indies, but **by 1805 Vice-Admiral Villeneuve was ready to attack**.

CHARISMA

Nelson, loved by his men, **took an active role, commanding from the front**, on deck, even after his secretary was shot in two.

0.69 IN. DIAMETER LEAD BALL
Nelson's fatal shot

THE DEATH OF NELSON

At **1:15 p.m. Nelson was hit by a shot from the French ship** *Redoubtable*, severing an artery in his lung and lodging in his spine. He was carried below as the battle raged on, Britain constantly surprising the French with changing tactics. At 1:30 p.m. the captain of the *Redoubtable* **surrendered, then at 2:15 p.m. Villeneuve surrendered**. Nelson **died shortly before 4:30 p.m.**

PUBLIC MOURNING

A flood of **national grief hit the public at the news**. Mourners filed past their hero's casket and, after a huge funeral procession, Nelson was **buried in the crypt of St. Paul's Cathedral**. To this day an **annual service and formal Trafalgar Night Dinner** are held in his memory.

15,000 mourners filed past Nelson's coffin; many more were turned away

104 guns on HMS *Victory*, the British Navy's flagship

2,890 rounds fired by HMS *Victory*

33 Vessels in the French Fleet

22 French ships lost

27 British ships

0 British ships lost

THE ROSETTA STONE

At first sight, this broken fragment of rock, densely engraved with strange symbols, seems insignificant, yet it has become a byword for the unraveling of mysteries.

TIMELINE

196 BC

Carved

JULY 15, 1799

Discovered

1801

Stone ceded to the British

1802

Presented to the British Museum

1917

Hidden in the underground Postal Railway during WWI

DISCOVERY

The stone was found in **Rosetta (Rashid), Egypt,** by soldiers in Napoleon's army. Commanding officer **Pierre-François Bouchard** realized how important it was.

WHAT DOES IT ACTUALLY SAY?
The Rosetta Stone is a **decree by priests from a temple in Memphis**, Egypt, supporting King Ptolemy V (ruled 204–181 BC).

WHY IS IT SO IMPORTANT?
The Rosetta Stone's message is **exactly the same in three languages**. Someone who could speak one of the languages could translate the others. Experts were finally able to translate hieroglyphs.

LANGUAGES

- **Demotic** (Egyptian everyday script)
- **Ancient Greek**
- **Hieroglyphs**, used mainly by ancient Egyptian priests

C.1818
English **Physicist Thomas Young** discovers some of the hieroglyphs on the stone **translate as a royal name: Ptolemy V**

1822
French scholar **Jean-François Champollion** pieces together a basic alphabet

1824
Using **Coptic**, similar to the demotic language, Champollion can now **fully read hieroglyphic inscriptions**

HEROES OF LATIN AMERICAN INDEPENDENCE

From a failed revolt in Venezuela in 1806 to the fall of the last Spanish garrisons in 1826, the collapse of the 300-year colonial rule of South America by Spain and Portugal was sudden and violent, as tension and resentment exploded into action.

SIMÓN BOLÍVAR

(1783–1830)

Charismatic military mastermind Bolívar, **a.k.a. "the Liberator,"** led the **revolution against the Spanish in Venezuela**, then continued via the **Battle of Boyacá**. There, **losing just thirteen men and fifty wounded, he killed 200 royalists and captured 1,600**. Bolívar eventually ruled over present-day Venezuela, Columbia, Ecuador, Peru, Panama, and Bolivia, but peace did not last long.

BERNARDO O'HIGGINS

(C.1776–1842)

Chile's national hero, gentleman farmer O'Higgins commanded the armies that would eventually **liberate Chile from Spain**, and became Supreme Director.

FRANCISCO DE MIRANDA

(1750–1816)

Although the **liberation of his homeland**—attempted by Venezuelan de Miranda in 1806—was **defeated, he became an inspiration for others**.

FATHER HIDALGO

(1753–1811)

When Miguel Hidalgo y Costilla – **a priest turned revolutionary**—was executed, he became a **symbol of Mexican independence.**

JOSÉ DE SAN MARTÍN

(1778–1850)

Argentinian by birth, San Martín **began as an officer in the Spanish army**, until he defected and **joined the revolutions against Argentina, Chile, and Peru**.

MANUELA SÁENZ

(1797–1856)

Originally from Ecuador, **Simón Bolívar's mistress** became "the Liberator of the Liberator" when she **saved Bolívar from assassins in 1828**.

THE REGENCY

When George III's mental health deteriorated beyond his ability to reign, his son—the future George IV—ruled as Regent.

 DATES 1810–20

 PUBLISHED AUSTEN'S *PRIDE AND PREJUDICE*, 1813

 BATTLE THE DUKE OF WELLINGTON DEFEATS BONAPARTE AT THE BATTLE OF WATERLOO, 1815, ENDING THE NAPOLEONIC WARS

 CASUALTIES THE PETERLOO MASSACRE, 1819, SEES FIFTEEN DEMONSTRATORS KILLED AND 400–700 INJURED

THE PRINCE REGENT

George was unpopular with the public, who hated his ostentatious lifestyle, **but his regency witnessed a flowering of arts, literature and style**.

BRIGHTON

Architect John "Beau" Nash remodeled the Prince's residence, in the small fishing town of Brighton, in the latest exotic **Indian and Chinese styles**. Delighted with his **Royal Pavilion**, the Prince took the fashionable set with him, leaving the previously favored city of Bath to invalids and elderly admirals.

JANE AUSTEN

Jane Austen's detailed accounts of **Regency life and etiquette** were from, in equal part, life and imagination.

FASHION

Women's high-waisted **"empire line"** dresses worked well with the sleek, simple lines introduced to men by dandy **Beau Brummel**. Brummel **rejected wigs and frock coats for breeches, tail coats**, and, famously, perfectly arranged neckties.

ARCHITECTURE

John Nash worked tirelessly for the Prince Regent, on new developments in London around the **Regent's Park**, **Regent's Street**, and **the Regent's Canal**.

AUSTEN'S PUBLISHED WORKS

- *Sense and Sensibility* (1811)
- *Pride and Prejudice* (1813)
- *Mansfield Park* (1814)
- *Emma* (1815)
- *Persuasion* (1817)
- *Northanger Abbey* (1817)

THE LAST FROST FAIR

Between 1309 and 1814 the Thames froze twenty-three times. Five of these occasions saw ice thick enough to bear a full-on, traditional frost fair.

 DATE FEBRUARY 1, 1814

 LOCATION THE RIVER THAMES, LONDON, ENGLAND

 ACTIVITY REVELING

 DURATION FOUR DAYS

FROZEN EUROPE

The Little Ice Age has no definitive timescale—most people agree plunging average temperatures hit the whole of northern Europe **between the sixteenth and nineteenth centuries**.

WHY DID THE RIVER FREEZE?

Under normal conditions **London Bridge**'s narrow arches created a mill-race effect, but **in extreme cold blocks of ice surging downstream snagged between the pillars, creating a dam**.

THE DARK SIDE

Pickpockets, **con men**, **prostitutes**, and **bookies** enjoyed rich pickings from folk snow-blind with frost fever.
Many Londoners, especially the poor, **froze or starved to death** or **fell through thin ice**.

FEASTING AND FUN

When watermen declared the ice safe, **hawkers hastily erected booths and stalls**, and **Londoners would flood onto the river** for a few days of **feasting**, **debauchery**, and **madness.**

SELFIES IN THE 1800S

Ten **ice-bound printing presses** printed, for a sixpence, small souvenir sheets with **partygoers' names**, **the date**, and **occasion**.

WHY DOESN'T THE THAMES FREEZE ANYMORE?

John Rennie's **new London Bridge**, opened in **1831**, boasted **fewer wider arches, keeping the Thames flowing. Joseph Bazalgette's 1862 embankments** contained the river, making it **narrower and deeper**.

ON THE MENU

Gingerbread
Hot apples
Sweetmeats and candies
Gin
Lapland mutton (regular sheep sold at a shilling a slice)
"Wellington For Ever: Good Ale"

SOUVENIRS

- Books and toys
- Knick-knacks
- Jewelry
- Cups and tankards

ENTERTAINMENT

- Jugglers
- Stilt walkers
- Sword swallowers
- Musicians

- Actors
- Acrobats
- Bull baiting
- Nine-pins
- Fox hunting

- Dancing
- Bowling
- Skating
- Gambling
- An elephant

THE BATTLE OF WATERLOO

When their armies finally clashed after twenty-odd years of bloody conflict, Napoleon and Wellington were each in personal command, yet the two would never actually meet.

DATE JUNE 18, 1815

LOCATION WATERLOO, BELGIUM

COMBATANTS BRITISH AND ALLIED ARMY, PRUSSIAN ARMY VS FRENCH IMPERIAL GUARD

RESULT BRITISH VICTORY; THE ALLIES ENTER PARIS JULY 7, 1815

BACKGROUND

Despite being beaten at Trafalgar, **Napoleon continued to invade much of Europe** before abdicating. On his return to Paris in **1815, Britain, Prussia, Russia and Austria declared war**.

DOWN BUT NOT OUT

On **June 16 Napoleon had defeated the Prussian Army at Ligny**. He did not know that, despite the Prussians' retreat, his enemy was still a fighting force to be reckoned with. **Wellington had just about held Quatre Bras, then fallen back to the village of Waterloo.** He decided to hold his ground until the Prussians arrived.

FATAL MISTAKE

Concerned the muddy ground would hamper progress, **Napoleon delayed the attack**, allowing Marshal Blücher's Prussian troops to come to the Allied army's aid.

TWO GIANTS

Each the same age and battle scarred with victories, **Napoleon and Wellington were well matched**. They had deep, if grudging, respect for one another.

CASUALTIES

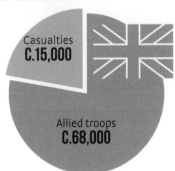

Casualties **C.15,000**

Allied troops **C.68,000**

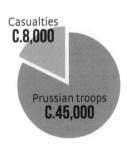

Casualties **C.8,000**

Prussian troops **C.45,000**

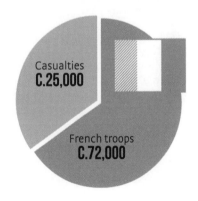

Casualties **C.25,000**

French troops **C.72,000**

THE BIRTH OF *FRANKENSTEIN*

Lord Byron, staying by Lake Geneva, challenges his friends to write a ghost story. At first uninspired, young Mary Shelley remembers a castle she's seen on her travels, and a monster is born.

TIMELINE

- **August 30, 1797** Mary Shelley is born

- **1816** Shelley writes a short story after experiencing "a waking dream"

- **1818** *Frankenstein; or The Modern Prometheus* is published by Lackington

- **1823** First stage adaptation

- **1831** First popular edition

- **1851** Mary dies

- **1910** First *Frankenstein* movie, directed by J. Searle Dawley

- **1931** Boris Karloff plays the monster

Mary was the **daughter of Mary Wollstonecraft**, radical author of *A Vindication of the Rights of Woman*, and **the philosopher William Godwin**. At sixteen **she eloped** with the (married) **poet Percy Bysshe Shelley**, traveling to Europe to avoid scandal.

SPOOF SPOOKS

Frankenstein parodies began almost immediately after the movie's release. Famous recent homages include *The Rocky Horror Picture Show*, *Frankenweenie* and *Young Frankenstein*.

SCIENTIFIC INSPIRATION

While inventing her crazed scientist's master plan, Mary remembered "animal electricity" experiments in Luigi Galvani and Giovanni Aldini's application of conducting rods to the cadavers of executed criminals.

A WOMAN'S TOUCH

At first everyone **believed** *Frankenstein* **was written by Percy Bysshe Shelley**. When they discovered it was by a woman, it was **downgraded to a "romance."**

500

The first print-run of *Frankenstein*

GOTHIC HORROR

The Gothic movement tapped into a romantic mood embracing **art**, **architecture**, and **literature**. By the early nineteenth century the genre was ridiculed by Jane Austen in *Northanger Abbey*, but Mary Shelley proved it could still chill.

THE RAILROAD AGE

The invention of the moving steam engine saw a revolution in transport. Britain's countryside was transformed as thousands of miles of track connected virtually every city, town, and village.

TIMELINE

- **1804** Richard Trevithick runs a steam locomotive along a track

- **1812** The first steam railroad train transports coal

- **1825** The Stockton and Darlington Railway becomes the first passenger railroad, pulled by George Stephenson's *Locomotion*

- **1829** George Stephenson's *Rocket* wins the Rainhill Trials race

- **1830** The Liverpool and Manchester Railway heralds a railroad-building boom

- **1836** London's first railroad is opened between Bermondsey and Deptford

- **1841** Thomas Cook runs the first railroad excursion

- **1847** Greenwich Mean Time is adopted by the railroads

- **1837** The London-to-Birmingham route becomes the first long-distance railroad

- **1863** The first underground railroad runs between Farringdon Street and Bishop's Road in London

- **1892** Standard gauge is adopted

EXPERIMENT

The first passenger carriage, *Experiment*, **was pulled by *Locomotion No.1*** on the Stockton and Darlington Railway.

Perishable goods could be safely transported in **hours rather than days**, bringing fresh food to the cities.

RAILROAD TIME

As long-distance rail became common, **local times were standardized** to keep schedules accurate.

THE GAUGE PROBLEM

If **more than one company ran a route** between cities, it was possible the **widths between tracks (gauge) at different points would vary**, meaning the same train couldn't complete the journey. Passengers and goods had to be **unloaded and reloaded** onto a different train.

HOLIDAYS AND EXCURSIONS

Railroads were able to transport people to the seaside for day trips. After **1871, four paid "bank holidays" were added** to Christmas Day, Good Friday, and Sundays (traditional days of rest), **allowing a break for millions**.

36	**15,000**	**24 MPH**	**650,000**	**272**
Wagons pulled by *Locomotion* on **September 27, 1825**	**Spectators** at the **Rainhill Trials**	**Top speed** of Stephenson's *Rocket*	**Passengers** on the London–Greenwich railroad in **15 months**	**Acts of Parliament** for proposed **railroad lines in 1846**

THE SLAVERY ABOLITION ACT 1833

The road to the end of slavery in Britain was long and hard. Too many people had made too much money to allow decency to get in the way of profit.

TIMELINE

- **1562** John Hawkins makes the first known slaving voyage to Africa

- **1772** A court rules that once in Britain, a slave cannot be forcibly returned to the colonies

- **1790** First abolition bill fails

- **1792** Second abolition bill fails

- **1794** France abolishes slavery

- **1804** A slave rebellion on Haiti establishes the first black state outside Africa

- **1807** The slave trade is abolished, but not slavery itself

- **1833** Abolition of Slavery Act passes

THE SLAVE TRIANGLE

Triangle ships never sailed empty . . .

Britain to Africa to pick up slaves, carrying textiles and rum

New World to Britain carrying sugar, tobacco and cotton

Africa to the New World carrying slaves

OLAUDAH EQUIANO

(1745–97)
Kidnapped and shipped to the New World, **Equiano managed to quietly buy his freedom**; his autobiography shocked London society.

GRANVILLE SHARPE

(1735–1813)
After befriending a slave who had been badly beaten by his master, Sharpe began to fight for the rights of **slaves who had been brought from the Caribbean to London**.

WILLIAM WILBERFORCE

(1759–1833)
Conversion to evangelical Christianity inspired the **Yorkshire MP to spend eighteen years fighting slavery**.

ELIZABETH HEYRICK

(1769–1831)
A leading female abolitionist, Heyrick **organized a sugar boycott in Leicester**.

SLAVE TRADE IN NUMBERS

C.10,000
British voyages to Africa, **enslaving about 3.4 million people** in the **245 years** between Hawkins's first voyage and the abolition of the slave trade.

12 MILLION
Estimated number of people transported by **European traders to the New World**.

80,000
Africans transported each year . . .

. . . 42,000
on British ships

THE SECOND VOYAGE OF THE *BEAGLE*

Despite crippling seasickness, Charles Darwin and his presence on board the British navy's survey ship HMS Beagle would change how we view the world forever.

 VESSEL HMS *BEAGLE*

 MISSION TO CIRCUMNAVIGATE THE GLOBE, MEASURING LONGITUDE

 DATES 1831–36

 CAPTAIN LIEUTENANT ROBERT FITZROY

 ON BOARD 68

 NATURALIST CHARLES DARWIN, TWENTY-TWO YEARS OLD

THE VOYAGE OF THE BEAGLE

In 1839 Darwin's account of his experiences was published as a book.

DECEMBER 27, 1831
The *Beagle* sets sail from Plymouth, England.

1832
At Santiago, Darwin **observes a band of shells in a cliff face**, 45 feet above sea level. How long had it taken to get there?

In Patagonia, **Darwin spends weeks collecting fossils**.

1833
On the **Falkland Islands**, Darwin realizes the **fossils are different** to those discovered earlier. He begins to wonder **how plants and animals**

have adapted to various environments.

At Punta Alt, Darwin sees a **skeleton embedded in layers of rock**. The creature must have died thousands of years ago.

Crossing the Rio Parana, Darwin **sees similar creatures to European animals**, conflicting with the idea that God created each species specifically for its own environment.

1834
Darwin **begins to think the planet must be constantly changing** rather than created in a single, perfect moment by God.

1835
At Villa Vincencio, Darwin sees **submarine lava flows** 6,000 feet above sea level. He realizes **the earth must be much older than the Bible says**.

1836
Seeing the **strangeness of the creatures in Australia**, Darwin thinks they must have been created separately.

On October 2, the *Beagle* docks at Falmouth.

FINCHES

Darwin became **fascinated by the various species of finch** he found in the Galapagos Islands, and many of his later studies concerned them.

DARWIN'S THIRD SHIPMENT HOME INCLUDED:

80 bird species
20 quadrupeds
4 barrels of skins and plants

LONG 19TH CENTURY 1789–1914

77

THE REIGN OF QUEEN VICTORIA

Princess Victoria's life was isolated and dominated by her overbearing mother. Queen Victoria defied bullying tactics, becoming her own woman—and one of Britain's longest-reigning queens.

 BORN MAY 24, 1819

 QUEEN JUNE 28, 1838

 MARRIED ALBERT OF SAXE-COBURG AND GOTHA, FEBRUARY 10, 1840

 WIDOWED DECEMBER 14, 1861

 EMPRESS OF INDIA MAY 1, 1876

 DIED JANUARY 22, 1901

ROYAL ENGAGEMENT

Deeply **in love with her first cousin Albert**, as monarch Victoria **had to propose to him**.

BLACK WIDOW

After Albert's death Victoria famously withdrew from public duties and ceremony, **dressing in black** and **relying on friends** for guidance. These included politician **Benjamin Disraeli**, **Scots ghillie John Brown**, and **Abdul Karim**, her 24-year-old Indian attendant.

CRIMEAN WAR

1853–56

In 1854 Britain, France, and Sardinia joined Turkey in a **bloody war against Russian expansionism**, fought on the Crimean peninsula.

THE BRITISH EMPIRE

Begun in the sixteenth century under Elizabeth I, **expansion in the nineteenth century brought more than a fifth of the world's land surface** and more than a quarter of its population under British control.

QUEEN MUM

Being Queen did not let Victoria off child-bearing duty. **She had nine children,** many of whom married into the great dynasties of Europe.

37

Number of grandchildren at her death

CHARLES DICKENS REINVENTS CHRISTMAS

Under the Georgians the grand medieval feast of Christmas had been reduced to a single day, usually celebrated by "rustics." Charles Dickens was having none of it. Written in just six weeks, his "little carol" changed a nation of Scrooges forever.

ORDER OF FESTIVITIES

1840 Queen Victoria marries Prince Albert

1843 *A Christmas Carol* is published the week before Christmas

1843 The first Christmas card is produced

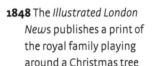
1848 The *Illustrated London News* publishes a print of the royal family playing around a Christmas tree

1848 Tom Smith invents the Christmas cracker

1840s onward Rail freight brings down the price of turkey

MID-LIST OBSCURITY

By **1843** "international superstar" **Dickens was struggling**. He had a mortgage and a fifth child on the way. **He needed a hit.**

6,000
Number of copies of *A Christmas Carol* sold within a few days

FIVE SHILLINGS
The book's original price

GHOST WRITER

Dickens wanted to find a palatable way to **highlight the poverty** he had seen on his travels. He wrote *A Christmas Carol* in the popular, time-honored, winter solstice tradition of the **ghost story**.

UNFAMILIAR CELEBRATIONS

The nostalgic celebrations Dickens describes **would have been alien to most people**. The Industrial Revolution had done away with the Twelve Days of Christmas and the **holiday was kept perfunctorily**. Readers, however, **loved the image Dickens portrayed, and chose to copy it**.

THE GREAT EXHIBITION

In 1851 Prince Albert, Queen Victoria's consort, oversaw a grand display of everything great about the British Empire. It was to prove the blueprint for a series of groundbreaking World's Fairs.

 DATES MAY 1–OCTOBER 11, 1851

 LOCATION HYDE PARK, LONDON

 VISITORS MORE THAN 6 MILLION, FROM ARISTOCRATS TO FACTORY WORKERS

 PRICE OF ADMISSION £3 FOR MEN, £2 FOR LADIES; FROM MAY 24 PEOPLE COULD ENTER FOR ONE SHILLING

 PROFIT £186,000 (£25.5 MILLION/ $33.2 MILLION TODAY)

 RESULT THE PROFITS WERE USED TO BUILD "ALBERTOPOLIS," A GROUP OF SOUTH KENSINGTON CULTURAL VENUES

WHY?

Albert wanted **to celebrate Britain being at peace**, undergoing a manufacturing boom, and **holding dominion over a large percentage of the world**.

THE CRYSTAL PALACE

Designed by Joseph Paxton and **built by Fox & Henderson** using iron and glass, the Crystal Palace was like a gigantic greenhouse. Its barrel-vaulted transept was **altered to accommodate three existing elm trees**.

ON DISPLAY

Exhibits displaying engineering, scientific, and artistic prowess came from across the world, but mainly Empire countries. They included:

- **A folding piano**
- Early bicycles
- **An ivory throne**
- An American eagle sculpture
- **A reaping machine**
- Sèvres porcelain
- **A knife with 80 blades**
- Cossack armor
- **Swiss watches**
- The Koh-i-noor Diamond
- **Stuffed kittens taking tea**
- A steam hammer

 ## RE-USE

After the exhibition, the **palace was reerected in Sydenham**, south London. It remained popular until 1936, when **it was gutted by fire**.

CRYSTAL PALACE IN NUMBERS:

| **1,848** ft. long / **408** ft. wide | **2** towers | **2,000** Estimated number of workmen by December 1850 | **1,000** iron columns | **4,000** tons of iron | **900,000** sq. ft. of glass |

THE AMERICAN CIVIL WAR

When seven slave-owning Southern states broke away from the Union, believing (correctly) that Lincoln would end slavery, their secession began a chain of devastating events.

 DATES 1861–65

 LOCATION MAINLY THE "BORDER STATES" BETWEEN THE TWO FACTIONS

 COMBATANTS NORTHERN UNION STATES VS SOUTHERN CONFEDERATE STATES

 RESULT REUNION; SLAVERY ABOLISHED

TIMELINE

1860

November 6 Lincoln elected President

December 20 South Carolina is the first Southern state to secede

1861

January/February Six more Southern states secede

March 4 Lincoln calls for peace but warns the Union must be retained

April 12 First gunfire, at Fort Sumter

April/May Virginia, Arkansas, Tennessee, and North Carolina secede

July 21 First major battle, Bull Run

1863

January 1 The Emancipation Proclamation declares all slaves free

July 1–3 Battle of Gettysburg; General Robert E. Lee's invasion of Pennsylvania is repelled

July 4 General Ulysses S. Grant splits the Confederate Army at the Siege of Vicksburg

November 19 *The Gettysburg Address*, where Lincoln presses for unity

1864

September 2 Confederate stronghold Atlanta is captured

1865

April 9 General Lee surrenders at the Appomattox Court House

December 18 The Thirteenth Amendment is ratified, abolishing slavery for all

WHAT CAUSED THE WAR?

The Northern states saw secession as unconstitutional. Lincoln's dedication to the **freedom of all men, including slaves**, was strong and he felt honor bound to preserve the Union, by force if necessary.

TECH

Both sides made **great use of modern technology**, including ironclads and submarines, telegraph and railroad, high-tech mines, hot air balloons, germ warfare, and photography.

620,000 Estimated deaths in the Civil War

THE ASSASSINATION OF ABRAHAM LINCOLN

By successfully prosecuting the Civil War from 1861–65, Abraham Lincoln earned the lasting enmity of many people in the South. He was the first U.S. President to be assassinated.

TIMELINE

MARCH
John Wilkes Booth starts plotting to kill the President

April 14 Lincoln is shot at Ford's Theatre, Washington, DC

Mortally wounded, Lincoln is taken to a nearby house; Booth and accomplice David Herold flee to Maryland

April 15 The President dies at 7:22 a.m.; Booth, wounded in the escape, stops to get his broken leg put in a splint

April 26 Booth and Herold are discovered; Booth is shot, Herold arrested

May 4 Lincoln is laid to rest

July 7 Four conspirators in the murder are executed by hanging

ABRAHAM LINCOLN

(BORN FEBRUARY 12, 1809)

Lincoln became **sixteenth President of the United States in 1861**. He had known hardship and felt injustice strongly. A **fierce advocate of the abolition of slavery**, he **warned the dissenting Southern states** that they were **forcing civil war by breaking away from the Union**, which he considered illegal. On his reelection **in 1864**, just as the war was ending, **he tried to make peace with the South**, but for some there was no forgiveness.

JOHN WILKES BOOTH

A **well-known actor, Wilkes Booth** became convinced Lincoln was responsible for the troubles of the South. He **thought he would be hailed a hero** for his actions. He was not.

OUR AMERICAN COUSIN

Wilkes Booth **knew where all the gags were** in this **hugely popular comedy**. He timed his shot to be covered by one of the **loudest laughs** of all.

THE TRANSCONTINENTAL RAILROAD

Fueled by the Gold Rush, the race to the West reached its zenith in the 1860s, as two rival companies vied to complete the first cross-country railroad.

TIMELINE

1830 First steam locomotive in America

1845 Asa Whitney proposes Congress fund an east–west railroad; he is refused

1849 Discovery of gold sees mass migration west

1860 Engineer Theodore Judah suggests the Donner Pass as a place to cross the Sierra Nevada mountain range

1861 The Central Pacific Railroad Company is formed

1862 The Pacific Railroad Act charters the Central Pacific and Union Pacific Railroad companies to link the United States from east to west

1863 Both companies begin but the Union side is held up until the end of the Civil War

1869 The two railroads meet at Promontory, Utah, on May 10

THE RACE

The Act stipulated that the **Central Pacific Railroad** would start building in **Sacramento, California**, **moving east** through the Sierra Nevada. The **rival Union Pacific Railroad Company** was to start at the **Missouri River, heading west**. The Act did not specify exactly where the two would meet.

To encourage swift construction, the **government promised 6,400 acres of land and $48,000 in government bonds ($1 million today) for every mile of track built**. Corners were cut and safety standards lapsed as each company vied to build as much as they could.

RESISTANCE

Native Americans, especially Sioux, Cheyenne, and Arapaho, feeling justifiably threatened, **attacked the works**.

LABOR

Both companies had difficulty retaining labor. **Some 14,000 Chinese workers were recruited in the west**; in the east laborers tended to be Irish immigrants.

GOING WEST

Before the railroad, travelers had to either **cross mountains**, plains, rivers, and deserts, **sail around Cape Horn**, or **cross the Isthmus of Panama**.

JOURNEY EAST TO WEST

$1,000
before 1869
($18,000 today)

$150
after 1869
($2,800 today)

9,000
miles of track east of the Missouri River by 1850, but nothing beyond

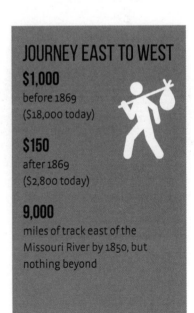

LOUIS PASTEUR AND THE FIGHT AGAINST GERMS

Pasteur discovered his love of chemistry as a teenager, but it was the deaths of three of his own children that prompted his war on disease.

TIMELINE

- **December 27, 1822** Born in Dole, France

- **1847** Receives doctorate

- **1849** Marries and has five children, but loses three to typhoid fever

- **1862** Invents Pasteurization

- **1885** Administers first vaccine

- **1888** Establishes the Pasteur Institute

- **September 28, 1895** Dies in Marnes-la-Coquette, France

GERM THEORY

People knew about microbes before Pasteur, but believed they occurred spontaneously. **Pasteur proved bacteria or "germs" were living organisms** that came from other living things.

DECAY

Pasteur began **observing the fermenting effects of mold and germs on perishable foods** such as wine and milk. He discovered that **most were killed by heat**, and developed a process we now know as **pasteurization**.

DISEASE KILLER

Pasteur realized a disease destroying silk worms was bacterial. **By destroying the silk worm bacteria, he saved the French silk industry.** He started to wonder if germs were the cause of human diseases, too.

SURGICAL SPIRIT

Thanks to Pasteur, **surgical instruments were boiled**, drastically **reducing deaths** on the operating table.

VACCINATION

Pasteur figured **a weak version of a disease** given to a healthy animal **would encourage its body to create antibodies**, making it immune to the real thing.

On **May 5, 1881**, **24 healthy sheep, 1 goat, and 6 cows were vaccinated** against anthrax. The same number were not vaccinated.

On **May 31**, all **62 animals were given anthrax**. Two days later the entire control group was dead or dying but **all the vaccinated animals remained alive**.

Pasteur turned to humans, **successfully treating nine-year-old Joseph Meister**, who had been **bitten by a rabid dog**.

PASTEUR'S PASTEURIZATION PROCESS IS STILL WIDELY USED TODAY, AND VACCINES CONTINUE TO SAVE MILLIONS OF LIVES

KARL MARX

Widely regarded as the father of Communism, Marx developed theories that became practice in several states during the twentieth century, including the Soviet Union and the People's Republic of China.

TIMELINE

- **1818** Born in Trier, Germany

- **1835** Begins to study Law

- **1841** Receives a doctorate from the University of Jena

- **1843** Moves to Paris, becomes revolutionary communist

- **1844** Begins collaborating with Friedrich Engels

- **1848** *The Communist Manifesto* is published

- **1849** Moves to London

- **1867** *Das Kapital* is published

- **1883** Dies and is buried in Highgate Cemetery

Marx's father had been **influenced by the Enlightenment**. Karl, born into a **Jewish** tradition, though **later baptized**, saw the role religion played in prejudice and discrimination. He also **saw the miseries inflicted on workers by the capitalist system**, and yearned for social justice.

MARX'S CHIEF INFLUENCES

GEORG HEGEL (1770–1831)
Hegel believed that history is linear, leading through **a series of trials until freedom is attained**.

LUDWIG FEUERBACH (1804–72)
Feuerbach believed religion exists as the consciousness of some kind of infinite presence within humans, implying **God is a projection of man's nature**.

FRIEDRICH ENGELS (1820–95)
Engels **collaborated with Marx** on *The Communist Manifesto*; Engels **edited** *Das Kapital*'s second and third editions after his friend's death.

COMMUNISM

Marx believed that the **abolition of private ownership**, as a result of class struggle, **would transform human nature, reconciling individual and community**. Production and distribution of goods and services would be **shared by the entire community, for the entire community**.

FREEDOM

Marx argued that **in a capitalist society the most valuable commodity was freedom**, especially the freedom to sell one's labor. **Engels clarified** this by saying **a truly classless society would exist to serve all humans**.

THE 1896 SUMMER OLYMPIC GAMES

In 1894 at a conference organized by Baron Pierre de Coubertin, it was decided that Athens, birthplace of the original Olympic Games, should host a grand revival.

 DATES APRIL 6–15, 1896

 LOCATION ATHENS, GREECE

 NATIONS ATTENDING 14

 EVENTS 43

 RESULT A HUGE SUCCESS, THE GAMES ARE STILL HELD EVERY FOUR YEARS

241 male athletes

0 female athletes

0 Paralympic athletes

60,000 spectators attended the first day

100,000 spectators watched the marathon

THE ANCIENT GAMES

Believed to have **originated in 776 BC**, **the first Olympics consisted of a single race run on foot between young men of Greek city-states** or colonies. Events were gradually added until **AD 393, when the games ceased**. Winners received olive branches and national glory. Winners were also given olive branches in the modern revival, along with silver medals.

PANATHENAIC STADIUM

Originally **built in 330 BC**, the ancient stadium was **rebuilt in white marble**.

FIRST MODERN MEDALLIST

American **James Connolly won the first event, the triple jump**, becoming the first Olympic Champion of modern times.

SWIMMING

Hungarian Alfréd Hajós won the 100 m race. For the **1,200 m**, swimmers were taken out a specific distance by boat and **expected to swim back to shore**. Alfréd Hajós won that, too.

MARATHON

The newly invented marathon race **followed the route** traditionally believed to have been taken by **ancient Greek runner Pheidippides**, when he brought news of victory from Marathon to Athens in 490 BC. Hugely significant to the people of Greece, the modern **race was won by a Greek athlete, Spyridon Louis**.

EVENTS INCLUDED

· Athletics · Cycling · Swimming
· Fencing · Wrestling · Shooting
· Tennis

MEDAL TABLE

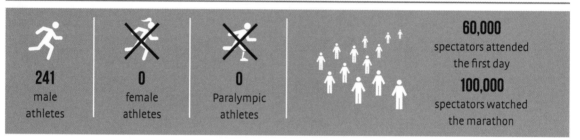

AMERICA **11** first-place finishes

GREECE **10** first-place finishes

GERMANY **6** first-place finishes

THE END OF THE SHOGUNS

The crowning of fourteen-year-old Prince Mutsuhito as 122nd Emperor of Japan marked the end of 200 years of isolation—and the rule of the Shoguns.

TIMELINE

1192 The Japanese Emperor gives military commander Minamoto Yoritomo the title "shogun"

1333 Ashikaga Takauji founds the second shogunate and builds the imperial city of Kyoto

1603 The powerful Tokugawa clan seizes power, ruling from the city of Edo

1853 U.S. Commodore Matthew Perry brings frigates and 1,500 soldiers; the Japanese are forced to trade with the U.S.; Britain, Russia, and France follow suit

1867 Crown Prince Mutsuhito becomes Emperor of Japan

1868 A group of samurai stage the Boshin War, a coup d'état ending the stranglehold of the Shoguns; Emperor Meiji moves to Edo and renames the city Tokyo

BACKGROUND

Samurai, Japan's warrior class, **began as provincial warriors hired to protect landowners battling for supremacy**. The victor pronounced his **top military commander "shogun."**

Shoguns gradually took total control, turning the **emperor into a token head of state**. Occasionally power would shift between rival *daimyo* (feudal lord) families, until one, the Tokugawa, dominated.

SAKOKU

Fearing European colonization, the **Tokugawa imposed "sakoku," or total isolation**.

THE CHARTER OATH

Mieji's first reform started the end of feudalism and **welcomed ideas from Europe**. Bureaucrats wrote a constitution and Japan began building an army, aiming to become the dominant force in the East.

MEIJI

The new period of rule, meaning **"enlightened rule."**

YELLOWSTONE NATIONAL PARK

Nineteenth-century America had a policy of transferring newly "discovered" public land to private ownership, but the wild, majestic beauty of Yellowstone persuaded Congress some things were too important to develop.

TIMELINE

Pre-1870 Native Americans live at Yellowstone for at least 11,000 years

1870 Explorers experience the fierce natural beauty of Yellowstone

1871 A Park Bill is read in Washington, drawing on the Yosemite Act of 1864 that reserves Yosemite Valley from settlement, becoming a State Park

1872 President Ulysses S. Grant signs the Yellowstone National Park Protection Act into law

1891 The National Forest System is established to preserve natural resources

1916 The origins of the National Park Service are founded

1918 Yellowstone gets its first park rangers

THE DIFFICULTIES

Yellowstone was huge and many people back east hadn't heard of it. **Why should this place be saved rather than any other?**

SEEING IS BELIEVING

William Henry Jackson's photographs, alongside **sketches by artists Thomas Moran** and Henry Elliott, were able to convey Yellowstone's grandeur, **catching public imagination**.

58
Number of national parks in the U.S. today

SPECIAL CASE

Yellowstone could not be a state park because it **crossed three territories: Montana, Wyoming, and Idaho.** Congress came up with a radical new plan: **national parks**.

The **1872 Act prohibited the settlement, occupancy, or sale** of any land within a specified area, setting it apart for the enjoyment of the people.

HOT COMPETITION

Hot Springs in Arkansas, set aside in 1832, is America's **oldest national reservation**, preserving a resource, hot water. It became a national park in 1921.

THE INVENTION OF THE LIGHT BULB

Thomas Edison is widely lauded as the inventor of the light bulb, but he should not take all the credit. Instead, inspired by the work of several inventors, Edison developed and, crucially, patented a light source that could work in every home.

TIMELINE

1802 British scientist Humphry Davy (1778–1829) invents the first electric light, the electric arc lamp

1840 British scientist Warren De la Rue (1815–89) passes a current through a coiled filament in a vacuum tube

1850 British scientist Joseph Wilson Swan (1828–1914) creates a "light bulb"

1874 Canadian electricians Henry Woodward and Matthew Evans try to commercialize their "electric lamp" but are unsuccessful

1878 Thomas Edison buys the patent and begins to research a practical electric light bulb

1880 Edison Electric Light Company launches the first commercial incandescent light bulb

1904 The tungsten filament is invented

1939 Fluorescent lamps are demonstrated at the New York World's Fair

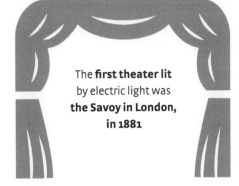

The **first house lit** by electricity was **Joseph Swan's, at Low Fell, Gateshead**

The **first theater lit** by electric light was **the Savoy in London, in 1881**

1,093 Patents registered by Thomas Edison in the United States

13.5 Hours Edison's bulb lasted in 1879

1,200 Hours Edison's improved "bamboo" filament bulb lasted in 1880

PARIS IN THE BELLE ÉPOQUE

France's "Beautiful Age" dates roughly from 1871 to 1914 and the outbreak of the First World War. Like the British Victorian and Edwardian eras and the American Gilded Age, it saw an unprecedented renaissance in everything from science to the arts.

LONG 19TH CENTURY 1789–1914

TIMELINE

- **1870–71** The Franco-Prussian War brings the collapse of the Second Empire

- **1871** The Paris Commune uprising; much of Paris is burned

- **May 1871** The Third Republic is declared

- **1872** Work begins on the Basilica of Sacré Coeur

- **1874** First exhibition by Impressionist painters

- **1875** Opera Garnier opens

- **1881** The Chat Noir cabaret opens in Montmartre

- **1889** The Eiffel Tower opens

- **1895** The Cordon Bleu cookery school opens

- **1895** The Lumière brothers present a projected moving picture show

- **1898** Louis Renault builds his first automobile

- **1900** Summer Olympics are held in Paris

- **1903** Pierre and Marie Curie receive a Nobel Prize for their work with radioactivity

- **1909** Louis Bleriot crosses the English Channel by plane

- **1913** Igor Stravinsky's "Rite of Spring" premieres

ART

Paris saw an explosion in experimental techniques, from **impressionists such as Auguste Renoir and Claude Monet** to **fauvists such as Henri Matisse** and **cubists including Pablo Picasso**. **Sculptor August Rodin** was hugely influential.

ARCHITECTURE

The curled, swirling lines of **art nouveau** penetrated both architecture, in buildings such as **Castel Béranger** and the **Paris Métro**, and design, with work from graphic artist Alphonse Mucha and **glass designer René Lalique**.

MUSIC AND LITERATURE

Writers such as Gustave Flaubert, Guy de Maupassant, Émile Zola, and Marcel Proust were balanced by experimental **composers including Claude Debussy and Georges Bizet,** whose opera *Carmen* was denounced as immoral.

POLITICAL UNREST

A **series of anarchist bombings** and disturbances by nationalists, agitating against Germany over the annexing of Alsace and Lorraine, meant the Époque was not always so Belle.

CHICAGO WORLD'S FAIR

1890s America was enjoying a golden age. Business was booming and railroads were distributing that wealth across the land. Every city wanted to host the World's Fair, but Chicago was determined to get it.

 DATE 1893

 LOCATION JACKSON PARK, CHICAGO

 OFFICIAL TITLE THE WORLD'S COLUMBIAN EXPOSITION

 CELEBRATING 400TH ANNIVERSARY OF COLUMBUS LANDING IN AMERICA

 ARCHITECT IN CHIEF DANIEL H. BURNHAM

The fair displayed **everything that was new and modern about the 1890s.** From the moment President Grover Cleveland pressed a button to power the new electric generator and illuminate the park, it was a hit.

Visitors entered via a brightly lit street to carnival barkers, music, and crowds. They witnessed **new inventions, performances,** and **new styles of art and culture.** Many of the wonders witnessed would become American classics in the next century.

THE WHITE CITY

The fair's centerpiece—Chicago's answer to London's Crystal Palace and Paris's Eiffel Tower—**was a "city" of neo-classical exhibition halls.**

THE DARK SIDE

Serial killer Herman Mudgett, a.k.a. Dr. H. H. Holmes, used the fair to find victims and cover his activities.

NOVELTIES AT THE WORLD'S FAIR

- Moving pictures • A Ferris Wheel
- Street lights • Belly dancers
- Carbonated soda • Camels
- Dishwashers • Shredded Wheat
- "Exotic" world music
- Juicy Fruit chewing gum
- Zippers

The fair told the world that **America had arrived.** More importantly, it told America, too.

THE WORLD'S FAIR IN NUMBERS

$10 MILLION
Guarantee put up by Chicago to host the exhibition

25 CENTS
Cost of watching construction

686 ACRES
Size of site

14
"Great Buildings" in the Beaux Arts style

65,000
Exhibits

7,000
Restaurant seating capacity

60 FT.
Uniform height of the classical buildings

27–28 MILLION
Attendees

$1 MILLION
Profit

C.25%
America's population visited the fair

THE DREYFUS AFFAIR

A seemingly small miscarriage of justice saw a wave of anti-Semitism flood nineteenth-century France and set a bitter seed that would grow twisted roots well into the twentieth century.

 13 X 13 FT. THE SIZE OF DREYFUS'S PRISON HUT

TIMELINE

1894 Ferdinand Walsin Esterhazy, a French major, starts selling military secrets to Germany

1895 Captain Alfred Dreyfus is found guilty of espionage; he is sentenced to life imprisonment on Devil's Island, French Guiana

1896 Evidence is discovered that Esterhazy is the real traitor; he is court-martialed, found guilty, and flees the country

1898 Famous writer Émile Zola publishes an open letter "J'Accuse" in *L'Aurore* newspaper, accusing the French government of a cover-up

1899 Dreyfus is tried again, found guilty again, but his sentence is commuted to ten years; after public outrage the French President pardons him

1906 Dreyfus is declared not guilty, reinstated and awarded the Legion D'Honneur

1995 The French Army publicly admits Dreyfus's innocence

LONG 19TH CENTURY 1789–1914

WHAT REALLY HAPPENED

French intelligence intercepted a message and realized **the spy must be on their staff**. Esterhazy and an accomplice **forged documents shifting the blame**. Suspicion fell on 35-year-old **Captain Alfred Dreyfus**, a Jewish officer from Alsace, who spoke German as his first language. **Anti-Semitism did the rest**.

TRIAL BY MEDIA

The Dreyfus Affair was one of the first played out in the media. Both sides used newspapers as weapons—the anti-Semitic paper *La Libre Parole* against the pro-Dreyfus *L'Aurore*.

The **public was split into Dreyfusards and anti-Dreyfusards**, with direct action on both sides. More than **fifty towns saw anti-Semitic riots**, while Dreyfusards threatened to boycott Paris's upcoming Universal Exposition.

RANK HUMILIATION

Before his deportation **Dreyfus was paraded through the streets and publicly stripped of his rank.**

DARK CLOUDS

The affair left a sour taste. **Dreyfus died in 1935** but five years later his wife had to go into hiding from the Nazis. Their **granddaughter was sent to Auschwitz**.

AROUND THE WORLD WITH NELLIE BLY

*Jules Verne's fictional Phileas Fogg traveled Around the World in 80 Days.
In 1889 two women from rival publications easily beat his time.*

TIMELINE

NOVEMBER 14, 1889, 9:40 A.M.

Elizabeth Bisland leaves New York City by train, heading west

JANUARY 30, 1890
Elizabeth Bisland arrives in New York, four days after Bly but still beating Fogg's time

Nellie Bly leaves New York City by steamship, heading east

JANUARY 25, 1890, 3:51 P.M.
Bly Arrives back in New Jersey

Elizabeth Cochran, writing as Nellie Bly, was one of America's first investigative reporters. She went undercover in a sweatshop and at New York's notorious Blackwell Island mental asylum, exposed unfair divorce laws, and even political corruption in Mexico.

PUBLICITY STUNT

A big fan of Jules Verne's 1873 novel, **Bly suggested to her editor** at the *New York World* **that she try to beat the fictitious record**. Not to be outdone, rival publication the *Cosmopolitan* hastily recruited its own intrepid explorer, **Elizabeth Bisland, who would circumnavigate the globe in the other direction**.

BACK HOME

The *World* kept readers interested by running a competition to guess Bly's exact timing. **She sent short reports by cable.**

TACTICS

The *World* slightly **cheated by chartering a nonstop, record-breaking "Miss Nellie Bly Special" train from San Francisco to Chicago**. *Cosmopolitan* allegedly bribed a steamer to wait for Bisland, but she managed to miss it.

BLY'S LUGGAGE

- An overcoat
- Underwear
- Toiletries
- £200 in gold and American dollars, in a bag around her neck

BOOKS

A Flying Trip Around the World
Elizabeth Bisland
1891

Around the World in Seventy-Two Days
Nellie Bly
1890

72 DAYS, 6 HOURS, 11 MINUTES AND 14 SECONDS
Nellie Bly's time

24,899
Miles covered

THE BOXER REBELLION

In 1900 the growing influence of the West and Japan on China led to violent attacks on foreigners and Chinese Christians by a group of organized rebels called the Society of the Righteous and Harmonious Fists (I Ho Ch'uan).

 DATES 1899–1901

 LOCATION SHANDONG PROVINCE, CHINA; LATER BEIJING

 COMBATANTS REBELS; LATER EMPRESS DOWAGER CIXI VERSUS THE EIGHT NATIONS

 CASUALTIES AN ESTIMATED 100,000 PEOPLE DIED IN THE REBELLION, WAR, AND RESULTING ANTI-BOXER ATROCITIES

 RESULT AFTER MUCH BLOODSHED, A PEACE AGREEMENT BETWEEN CHINA AND THE EIGHT NATIONS

BACKGROUND

China's ruling **Qing dynasty** had been **weakened by the Opium Wars of 1839–42**, which had forced China to trade with the rest of the world. By 1899 attacks on foreign diplomats, missionaries, and merchants were common. **Emperor Guangxu tried to modernize China too fast and resentment was rife.**

SECRET SOCIETY

The Righteous Fist society consisted mainly of peasants, dogged by famine, drought, and floods. They **blamed the influx of foreigners for their wretched state**.

Members of the society **practiced martial arts and traditional spiritualism**. Westerners **described their activities** using the closest term they understood—**boxers.**

ATTACKS

Boxers rampaged through Shandong throughout 1900, killing foreigners and burning churches. They cut the railroad line, isolating Beijing, buoyed by the support of proxy-ruler Empress Dowager Cixi.

THE EIGHT NATIONS

An **alliance was made** from countries with trading interests in China: **Austria–Hungary, France, Germany, Italy, Japan, Russia, the United States**, and **Great Britain**. Peace was finally attained—at horrific cost.

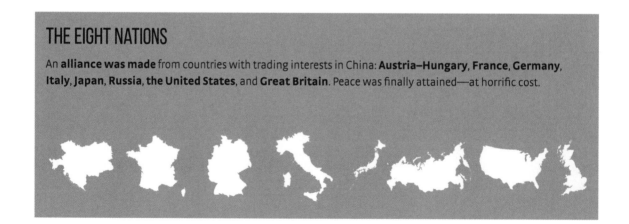

THE INVENTION OF THE AUTOMOBILE

The concept of a self-propelling carriage has appealed to humans since ancient times. Even Leonardo da Vinci came up with ideas for one. Many minds have taken the dream to reality and no one inventor can claim sole ownership.

SOME EARLY IDEAS FOR PROPULSION:

- Coiled springs
- Clockwork
- Windmills
- Air pumps
- Vacuums
- Steam
- Gas

STEAM

1769

In **France, Nicolas-Joseph Cugnot invented a steam tricycle** running at 2.25 mph. **Steam** was exploited throughout the eighteenth and nineteenth centuries, including in lightweight, personal steam carriages, but was **ultimately too heavy and cumbersome**.

GASOLINE

An **internal combustion engine** uses the explosion caused by sparking an oxidizer with fuel, to move pistons or other moving parts. Like all car components, **it evolved slowly**. The **first commercial product was patented by Jean Joseph Étienne Lenoir in 1860**. He built a three-wheeled, gasoline-driven carriage in 1863.

Karl Benz presented his first motor car in 1885. Fellow German Gottlieb **Daimler's version appeared in 1886**.

Dozens of companies and individuals now worked on many models in both Europe and America.

The first recognizably modern car was the 1901 Mercedes, produced by Daimler Motoren Gesellschaft. The same year, **in the U.S., Ransom E. Olds produced** the first mass-produced car, **the Curved Dash Oldsmobile** at the relatively cheap price of $650 ($19,200 or £14,700 today).

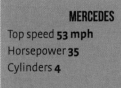

In 1908 Henry Ford produced his Model T. Unassuming, uncomfortable, reaching modest speeds, and available only in black, it was, however, both **practical and affordable**. Using production-line factories, he shaved the price from $850 ($23,200 or £17,800 today) to under $300 by 1925 ($4,300 or £3,300 today).

15 MILLION+
Model T cars produced between 1913 and 1927

MERCEDES		OLDSMOBILE
Top speed **53 mph**		Top speed **20 mph**
Horsepower **35**		Horsepower **3**
Cylinders **4**		Cylinders **1**

HUNDREDS OF COMPANIES BEGAN DESIGNING VEHICLES, ATTEMPTING TO COMBINE THE **EFFICIENCY OF THE MERCEDES** WITH THE **PRICE OF THE OLDSMOBILE**

THE TRIAL OF OSCAR WILDE

Even in a world where "the love that dare not speak its name" was considered "gross indecency," Oscar Wilde thought he would win his libel case. Instead he found himself in the dock.

In 1891 the celebrated Irish wit, poet, and playwright met Lord Alfred Douglas, sixteen years his junior. **Douglas's father**, the powerful Marquess of Queensberry, **disapproved of their secret relationship**.

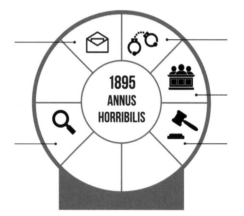

1895 ANNUS HORRIBILIS

February 18, 1895 Wilde receives an offensive card at his club, addressed to the "posing sodomite." Against his friends' advice he pursues the Marquess for libel

April 3 The trial begins; the Marquess hires private detectives to prove his case

April 6 Wilde arrested for gross indecency

April 26 In a packed court Wilde pleads "not guilty"

May 25 Wilde is convicted and sentenced to two years' incarceration with hard labor

WILDE'S PRISONS

After being processed at **Newgate**, Wilde was moved to **Pentonville** and **Wandsworth prisons**, before finishing his sentence at **Reading Gaol**.

NEWGATE   PENTONVILLE

WANDSWORTH   READING

HARD LABOR

Suffering from **dysentery and malnutrition**, Wilde spent hours walking a treadmill and **"picking oakum" (unraveling rope)**.

FREEDOM—OF A SORT

Wilde was released in 1897, depressed, in poor health, and with a perforated eardrum. **He died in 1900.**

SWANSONG

Wilde's *The Ballad of Reading Gaol*, written in exile in France, describes the **experiences of a prisoner on death row, awaiting execution**.

THE WRIGHT BROTHERS' FIRST FLIGHT

In 1903 Wilbur and Orville Wright became the first to fly a heavier-than-air machine that took off under its own power, remained under control, and sustained flight.

 DATE DECEMBER 17, 1903

 LOCATION KITTY HAWK, NORTH CAROLINA

 CRAFT *THE WRIGHT FLYER*

 TYPE BIPLANE

 WEIGHT 625 LBS. (750 LBS. WITH PILOT)

THE WRIGHT BROTHERS

The brothers, from **Dayton, Ohio**, had already designed a successful glider. **When no company could supply a suitable engine, they built their own.**

THE FLYER

3 SPECIAL CONTROLS:
wing-warping for balance, a moveable rudder for steering, and an elevator for pitch control

1 wing shorter than the other to compensate for engine weight

12 horsepower

4 flights

THE GRAND JUNCTION RAILROAD

The brothers built a **60 ft. launching rail** along which the *Flyer* ran on a wheeled truck.

The brothers **tossed a coin to see who would take the first trip**.

3.5 SECONDS

FLIGHT 1
December 14
Wilbur keeps *Flyer* airborne for 3.5 seconds

12 SECONDS

FLIGHT 2
December 17
Orville makes the first proper flight for 12 seconds

12 SECONDS

FLIGHT 3
December 17
Wilbur makes a similar flight

15 SECONDS

FLIGHT 4
December 17
Orville manages 15 seconds

59 SECONDS

FLIGHT 5
December 17
Wilbur flies for 59 seconds

WOMEN'S SUFFRAGE

In 1832 Henry Hunt presented a petition to Parliament on behalf of spinster Mary Smith of Yorkshire. She felt that as she paid taxes, she should be allowed to vote. Her bid failed but set minds thinking.

TIMELINE

1897 The **National Union of Women's Suffrage Societies** formed

1903 The **Women's Social and Political Union (WSPU)** formed

1907 **76 suffragettes arrested** trying to storm the **Houses of Parliament**

1908 Women's Sunday demonstration attracts **250,000 protestors**

1909 **Marion Wallace Dunlop** goes on **hunger strike** in prison, starting a trend; later that year, **prisons force-feed inmates**

1910 After a bill is passed but fails to become law, a **WSPU march is brutally put down**

1911 **Emily Wilding Davison (1872–1913)** hides in a cupboard in the Houses of Parliament on census night

1913 The **Cat and Mouse Act** releases prisoners on hunger strike then rearrests them; **Emily Wilding Davison is killed when she steps in front of the King's horse** at the Epsom Derby

1914 **Emmeline Pankhurst (1858–1928)** attempts to **present a petition to the King**; outbreak of war temporarily halts the campaign

1918 **Representation of the People Act passed**, allowing women to vote if over thirty and registered property owners

1919 **Nancy Astor** takes her seat as the **first female MP in Britain**

1928 **Representation of the People (Equal Franchise) Act** allows everyone over the age of twenty-one to vote

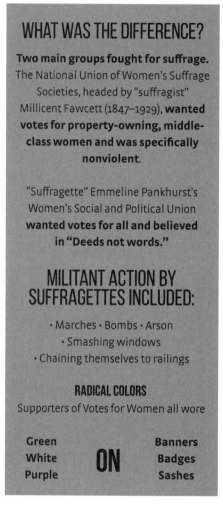

WHAT WAS THE DIFFERENCE?

Two main groups fought for suffrage. The National Union of Women's Suffrage Societies, headed by "suffragist" Millicent Fawcett (1847–1929), **wanted votes for property-owning, middle-class women and was specifically nonviolent.**

"Suffragette" Emmeline Pankhurst's Women's Social and Political Union **wanted votes for all and believed in "Deeds not words."**

MILITANT ACTION BY SUFFRAGETTES INCLUDED:

· Marches · Bombs · Arson
· Smashing windows
· Chaining themselves to railings

RADICAL COLORS
Supporters of Votes for Women all wore

Green		Banners
White	ON	Badges
Purple		Sashes

MEMBERSHIP OF WOMEN'S SUFFRAGE SOCIETIES IN 1914

WSPU 5,000

NUWSS 50,000

THEODORE ROOSEVELT

The 26th President of the United States was also the youngest to take office, at just forty-two.

TIMELINE

- **October 27, 1858** Born in New York City

- **1880** Graduates from Harvard University

- **1882** Elected to the New York State Assembly; he will serve two terms

- **1884** Roosevelt's wife and mother die on the same day; grieving, he spends two years on a ranch in Dakota

- **1886** Returns to New York City and remarries

- **1898** On the outbreak of the Spanish–American War, Roosevelt becomes colonel of the First U.S. Volunteer Cavalry, a.k.a. the Rough Riders

- **1901** Becomes President after the assassination of William McKinley

- **1901** Shocks society by inviting Booker T. Washington to dinner, the first black guest entertained by a President at the White House

- **1903** Helps facilitate secession of Panama from Colombia, paving the way for construction on the Panama Canal

- **1904** Reelected

- **1904–5** Helps negotiate peace in the Russo-Japanese War

- **1912** Bids for the presidency under the Progressive Party, a.k.a. The Bull Moose Party. The Republican Party split sees the Democrats win

- **January 6, 1919** Dies in Oyster Bay, New York

OUTDOORS TYPE

Roosevelt was a sickly child, who invented himself a program of tough physical exercise. He became strong, and a **great lover of nature and the Wild West**.

TRUST BUSTER

In his **"Square Deal" program**, Roosevelt made headway in **breaking up monopolist business practices** using the **1890 Sherman Antitrust Act**.

PEACEMONGER

Roosevelt **won the coveted Nobel Peace Prize** after negotiating the **end of the Russo-Japanese War**.

200 MILLION ACRES

set aside for **national forests**, **reserves**, and **wildlife refuges** under Roosevelt's presidency

TEDDY BEARS

Despite being a **notorious big-game hunter**, in 1902 Roosevelt **refused to shoot a tethered bear**, as it was unsportsmanlike. Plush **"Teddy's Bears" were invented by Morris Michtom** and his wife Rose to remember the occasion.

MADAM C. J. WALKER

Women, especially women of color, didn't often go into business in the early years of the twentieth century. Madam C. J. Walker not only became the first female American self-made millionaire, she created a way out of poverty for hundreds more African American women.

TIMELINE

December 23, 1867 Sarah Breedlove was born, the first free child of former slaves

Age 7 Orphaned

Age 14 Marries to escape abusive brother-in-law

Age 20 Widowed

Age 22 Moves to St. Louis, Missouri, to work as a laundress and cook

Age 27 Marries again, then divorces

Age 38 Marries again and launches her own hair products, under her married name Madam C. J. Walker

HAIRY TIMES

As a woman with scalp problems herself, Walker understood bad hair days

$1.50
Sarah Breedlove's daily wage as a washerwoman

THE WALKER SYSTEM OF HAIR CULTURE

The system involved **special brushing techniques**, heated combs, and her own-recipe **Wonderful Hair Grower**.

She began a **mail order business**, then—after divorcing a second time—**built a factory** in Indianapolis and **opened a beauty school** for her licensed sales agents.

40,000
Number of **African Americans Madam C. J. Walker employed** in the U.S., Central America, and the Caribbean.

CHARITY WORK

Walker **moved to Harlem in 1913**, where she immersed herself in philanthropic deeds. **She gave huge sums of money to charity**, including $5,000 ($72,500 or £55,500 today) **to the National Association** for the Advancement of Colored People's antilynching fund.

She died in 1919, **the sole owner of a business valued at more than $1 million** ($14.5 million or £11.1 million today).

Average wages per week

Madam Walker's workers $10

Southern workers $2

THE DISCOVERY OF MACHU PICCHU

Staggering up a drizzle-drenched mountain on July 24, 1911, explorer Hiram Bingham III thought he had been duped about what he would find. Reaching the top, however, he was dazzled by an ancient, ruined city in the clouds.

 7,972 FT. above sea level

 8,923 FT. to the peak of Huayna Picchu

3 FAMILIES of farmers lived on site when Bingham arrived

20 buildings were visible

500 buildings were revealed by excavations

1983 the year UNESCO appointed Machu Picchu a World Heritage Site

THE INCA EMPIRE

The **Incas were skilled in architecture, engineering**, and **military prowess** but they were no match for conquistador Francisco Pizarro, who coveted their gold. **Spanish guns, horses—and diseases—devastated the once-great empire.**

PERU

EXPEDITION

Bingham came in search of the lost citadel Vilcabamba, where the last of the Incas were defeated in 1572. A local farmer, Melchor Arteaga, promised something spectacular.

Bingham was, indeed, astounded, but more would come. **Grain stores, terraces, houses, palaces, fountains, canals,** and **the astonishing Temple of the Sun,** arranged to catch the sun's rays on winter solstice, would all fetch up in later excavations. **Until his death Bingham believed he had found Vilcabamba.**

The Spanish never knew about Machu Picchu, so there were no records of it. It is **believed to have been the mountain retreat of the fearsome fifteenth-century Inca warrior-emperor Pachacuti.**

RACE TO THE SOUTH POLE

By the early twentieth century few places on earth remained undiscovered. In 1911 two teams, one each from Great Britain and Norway, set out to reach the South Pole.

NORWAY

 TEAM LEADER ROALD AMUNDSEN

 SHIP *FRAM*

 LEFT BASE CAMP OCTOBER 18, 1911

 ARRIVED AT POLE DECEMBER 14, 1911

 RETURNED TO BASE CAMP JANUARY 25, 1912

GREAT BRITAIN

 TEAM LEADER ROBERT FALCON SCOTT

 SHIP *TERRA NOVA*

 LEFT BASE CAMP NOVEMBER 1, 1911

 ARRIVED AT POLE JANUARY 17, 1912

 RETURNED TO BASE CAMP NEVER

AMUNDSEN

(1872–1928)

A respected explorer, **Roald Amundsen kept his plans secret**. He took a **different route and made base camp 60 miles further south than Scott**, whose motorized equipment had failed. He took four men for the final push for the Pole, against Scott's five, meaning rations were less stretched.

SCOTT

(1868–1912)

Scott had already made one attempt on the Pole, in 1901–04, failing but setting a new record. He was determined to try again.

SCOTT'S TEAM SUFFERED FROM

- Exhaustion
- Starvation
- Gangrene
- Hypothermia
- Scurvy
- Frostbite

£20,000 Grant Scott received from the British Admiralty (£2.3 million today)

Scott's team died **11 MILES** from supply camp

52 DOGS used by Amundsen in the final push

THE RACE IS ON

Stopping at Australia, Scott received a **telegram** from Amundsen informing him he was also aiming for the Pole.

THE POLE

Exhausted, gravely ill, and forced to abandon their motor sledges, Scott's team dragged supplies themselves. Arriving at the Pole, they found Amundsen's flag already planted there.

THE END

Petty Officer **Edgar Evans died on February 17** after slipping behind the group. **Captain Lawrence Oates**, realizing he was a drain on supplies, left his tent in a blizzard on **March 17**, his 32nd birthday. The final three team members—**Scott, Edward Wilson, and Henry Bowers—died on or soon after March 29, 1912.**

THE SINKING OF RMS *TITANIC*

At 11:40 p.m. on Sunday, April 14, 1912, RMS Titanic struck an iceberg.
By midnight, six watertight compartments had been breached. Four days into
the crossing from Ireland to New York, Titanic was going to sink.

 RMS *TITANIC* THE "UNSINKABLE" SHIP

 CONSTRUCTION BUILT BY THE WHITE STAR LINE, COMPETITORS OF CUNARD, WHICH HAD SET SPEED RECORDS CROSSING THE ATLANTIC

 COST $7.5 MILLION ($167 MILLION TODAY)

 WEIGHT 46,000 TONS

 MAX PASSENGERS AND CREW 2,603 PASSENGERS, 944 CREW

 LIFEBOATS 16 + 4 COLLAPSIBLE (1,178 CAPACITY)— HALF THE PASSENGERS

CAPTAIN SMITH

- Edward J. Smith was known as **"the millionaire's captain."** He was the number-one choice for aristocrats of the day.
- Smith was placed in command of *Titanic*, despite **two accidents** involving ships under his command **in 1911**.
- Many myths surround the captain, the most famous being that **he ignored ice warnings**.
- Witnesses reported **he dived into the sea** as the bridge of the ship went under.

TITANIC IN NUMBERS

Approximately 2,200 people were on board

900 CREW
1,300 PASSENGERS
IT WAS LESS THAN **75%** FULL

Of the passengers . . .

324 1ˢᵀ CLASS
284 2ⁿᴰ CLASS
709 3ᴿᴰ CLASS

 **37** SECONDS

. . . elapsed between the sighting of the iceberg and the collision

20 lifeboats were enough for **HALF of the passengers**

Only **700** people made it onto a lifeboat—most left with empty seats

THE GLAMOUR OF TITANIC

The **ship's interiors** were inspired by the Ritz in London.

THE RITZ

First-class passengers were able to enjoy reading rooms, a palm court, gymnasium, swimming pool, squash court, Turkish baths, and a barber shop.

AFTERMATH

Only **306** bodies were found

The wreckage was discovered in 1985, **370 miles** off the coast of Newfoundland. The bow penetrated **18 meters into the seabed**.

The last remaining survivor, Millvina Dean, was **two months old** when the ship sank. She died on May 31, 2009, **aged 97**.

THE PANAMA CANAL

Before 1914 ships wishing to sail between the Atlantic and Pacific oceans were forced to make the long, dangerous journey around Cape Horn in South America.

 PANAMA CANAL A LOCK-TYPE CANAL CONNECTING TWO OCEANS

 LATITUDE 9°N

 RUNS DUE SOUTH FROM COLÓN (ATLANTIC) TO BALBOA (PACIFIC)

 LENGTH 40 MILES SHORELINE TO SHORELINE; 50 MILES DEEP WATER TO DEEP WATER

LONG 19TH CENTURY 1789–1914

TIMELINE

- **16th century** Spanish begin to talk of the possibilities of a canal

- **1881** Ferdinand de Lesseps, from France, who had developed the Suez Canal, attempts a second channel across the Isthmus of Panama

- **1898** De Lesseps is forced to abandon the project; offers the construction for sale

- **1902** The Spooner Act is passed by U.S. Congress, purchasing the project, but fails to make a treaty with Colombia

- **1903** Panama declares independence

- **1904** The Hay–Bunau–Varilla Treaty allows the U.S. to build

- **August 15, 1914** The canal is opened

- **1977** The Panama Canal Treaty begins to bring the canal back under Panamanian control

- **1999** The U.S. hands control to Panama; the Neutrality Treaty guarantees permanent neutrality of the canal, with nondiscriminatory tolls and access for all nations

- **2016** Expansion work is complete

LOCKS

To create a **sea-level channel would have proved costly**, so the French decided on a lock-based system.

PANAMANIAN INDEPENDENCE

Panama was, until 1903, part of Colombia. With U.S. backing, it declared itself independent.

PRICE OF INDEPENDENCE

$10,000,000 OUTRIGHT FEE + $250,000 ANNUITY
The settlement Panama received for permission to build and govern the canal

25,600 Estimated number of lives lost building the canal

2 ROUTES CONSIDERED
Panama and Nicaragua

8–10 HOURS
Average time it takes to pass through the canal

164 SQ. MILES
Surface area of Gatún, then the largest artificial lake in the world, created to make the locks work

The Panama Canal can shorten a ship's voyage by **8,000 NAUTICAL MILES**

THE ASSASSINATION OF ARCHDUKE FERDINAND

In 1914 Europe was spoiling for war; all it needed was a match to the tinderbox. A small group of assassins literally lit a fuse.

TIMELINE

JUNE 28, 1914

9:30 a.m. The Archduke and his wife Sophie, Duchess of Hohenberg, are met by Governor Potiorek at Sarajevo station

10:10 a.m. Nedjelko Čabrinović throws a hand grenade at the Archduke's car; it bounces off the hood and explodes under the car behind

10:20 a.m. The Archduke demands to visit the injured in hospital

10:50 a.m. The car takes a wrong turning; as it turns around, Gavrilo Princip shoots Franz Ferdinand and Sophie

11:30 a.m. Sophie is dead on arrival at the Governor's house; Franz Ferdinand dies a few minutes later

VICTIMS

About **twenty people were injured by the bomb**.

The **second bullet was intended for Governor Potiorek** but went astray in a tussle.

FRANZ FERDINAND & SOPHIE, DUCHESS OF HOHENBERG

BACKGROUND

Bosnia had been annexed from Serbia by Austria–Hungary, a German ally. **Bosnian nationalists**, who wanted freedom, **found sympathy in Serbia**, which was allied with the Russian Empire. When Archduke Franz Ferdinand, **heir to the Austrian throne**, announced a trip to Sarajevo, **the assassins assembled**.

THE BLACK HAND

7 **young Bosnian Serb conspirators** received bombs and guns from the Black Hand, **a Serb terrorist organization**.

AFTERMATH

Too young for the death penalty, **both Nedjelko Čabrinović and Gavrilo Princip were sentenced to twenty years in prison** but died of tuberculosis in 1916 and 1918 respectively.

CONSEQUENCES

The government of **Austria–Hungary saw the assassinations as a direct attack**, believing the Serbians to be behind it. **Russia began to mobilize to back up Austria**. Austria–Hungary declared war on Serbia, and **Germany declared war on Russia to help its ally**. France began to help Russia, and so Germany declared war on France.

The First World War had begun.

GALLIPOLI

The Gallipoli campaign, a.k.a. the Dardanelles campaign, was one of the most tragic events of the First World War.

 DATES FEBRUARY 1915–JANUARY 1916

 LOCATION DARDANELLES STRAITS AND GALLIPOLI PENINSULA, TURKEY

 COMBATANTS ALLIED POWERS VS OTTOMAN EMPIRE

 CASUALTIES 500,000 ACROSS BOTH SIDES

 RESULT ALLIED FAILURE

NAVAL BATTLE

On February 19, 1915, **British and French ships failed to capture the Dardanelles Straits**, which connected the Aegean Sea with the Sea of Marmara.

LAND INVASION

- On **April 25 Allied troops landed at Cape Helles and Ari Burnu, later renamed Anzac Cove**. They met powerful opposition from the Turkish Army and suffered huge losses.

- Another **landing on August 6 gave the Allies a brief advantage**, but they wasted it in delays caused by indecision.
- **Trench warfare saw troops unable to advance.** Hungry, sick, surrounded by the bodies of their compatriots and swarms of black flies, the soldiers sank into diseased stalemate.
- Commander Sir Ian Hamilton was replaced by Sir Charles Munro. Faced with little choice, the **Allies began to evacuate the 105,000 troops on December 7**.

ALLIED TROOPS FROM:

- Australia
- New Zealand
- France
- Britain

480,000 Allied troops took part

ANZAC

The Australian New Zealand Army Corps was formed in Egypt in 1914; the term **"Anzac" eventually meant any Australian or New Zealand soldier**.

REMEMBRANCE

Back in Britain, the military and human disaster led to Prime Minister Asquith's resignation. In Australia and New Zealand, the scars still run deep. **Each April 25, Anzac Day honors the soldiers who didn't come home.**

CASUALTIES:
250,000
suffered on each side, of which…

ALLIES
46,000–58,000 dead

TURKISH
87,000 dead

29,000
British and Irish

11,000
Australian and New Zealanders

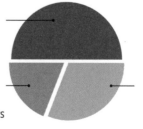

18,000
Other

THE BATTLE OF THE SOMME

The largest battle of the First World War, the Somme was also one of the bloodiest battles of any war, before or since. It was a joint operation between British and French forces to achieve victory over the Germans on the Western Front.

 DATES JULY 1–NOVEMBER 19, 1916

 LOCATION THE BANKS OF THE SOMME RIVER, FRANCE

 COMBATANTS BRITAIN AND FRANCE VS GERMANY

 CASUALTIES BRITAIN: 420,000; FRANCE: 200,000; GERMANY: 600,000

RESULT STALEMATE

PREBATTLE

- Before the battle was launched, British troops massed at the Somme for a **seven-day artillery bombardment**.
- The army **fired over 1,700,000 shells** at the German trenches.
- **Only the heaviest artillery had any effect** on the German defenses, and the quick breakthrough that the British hoped for was not achieved.

THE MEN WHO FOUGHT

750,000 men from **twenty-seven divisions** went into the attack, of which **over 80 percent were from the British Expeditionary Force** (BEF).

WHAT WAS ACHIEVED?

- Over the next **141 days**, the British advanced a maximum of **7 miles**.
- Despite the devastating losses, it was **ultimately a strategic victory** and hurt the Germans very badly.

REMEMBRANCE

- The Commonwealth War Graves Commission maintains more than **450 memorials and cemeteries** in the Somme region.
- **The Thiepval Memorial** to the Missing of the Somme lists 72,195 names of men **with no known grave**.

THE FIRST DAY

At **7:20 a.m. on July 1**, a

LARGE MINE

was detonated under Hawthorn Ridge. **Ten minutes later**, the infantry went over the top.

The British advanced at a **walking pace**, partly due to lack of training for the men, and partly because they were weighed down by **66 lbs. of equipment**.

On the first day,

19,240

British soldiers lost their lives.

The battalion from the island of Newfoundland, now part of Canada, suffered the heaviest losses:

90%

of their **2,000 men** on the opening day of the battle.

MILITARY HONORS

51 **soldiers** from the Commonwealth and Empire armies were **awarded the Victoria Cross** for their services during the battle.

THE DEATH OF RASPUTIN

*During his lifetime, mystic Grigori Rasputin held the Russian royal family
in his thrall. In death, his story captivates the world.*

  DATE DECEMBER 30, 1916

LOCATION THE PALACE OF PRINCE FELIX YUSUPOV,
ST. PETERSBURG

 ASSASSINS PRINCE YUSUPOV AND VLADIMIR PURISHKEVICH

BACKGROUND

Czar Nicholas II of Russia and
Czarina Alexandra had a deadly
secret: **their only son and heir,
Alexei, suffered from hemophilia.**
His blood could not clot, leaving him,
potentially, to bleed to death.

THEM THERE EYES

Fanatical mystic **Grigori Rasputin's
wild looks were terrifying**
enough for the newspapers, but his
haunting, demon-like eyes turned
him into the stuff of nightmares.

**The desperate Romanovs
believed Rasputin could cure
their son**, but the public saw only a
sinister man with a strange power
over the royal couple—and, if things
weren't stopped, Russia itself.

THE DEATH OF RASPUTIN

The Czar left the Czarina in charge while he went to fight the First World War.
Fearing Rasputin would take even more power, conspirators decided he had to go.

Eyewitness accounts of Rasputin's final hours vary wildly
and Prince Yusupov's account is contested:

The mystic
is lured to a
basement, where
he is **poisoned
with cakes** to
seemingly no
effect

**Yusupov shoots
Rasputin**; he
falls to the
ground "dead"
and conspirators
leave the room

Conspirators
return; Rasputin
has staggered
into a courtyard

He is shot "dead,"
then begins to
twitch; **he is
bludgeoned
with a mallet**

**Rasputin
was buried secretly**
and **visited by the
Czarina** until the
Romanovs' arrests by the
Bolsheviks, two months
later. **The body was
disinterred, burned,
and the ashes
thrown to
the wind.**

The corpse is thrown into the Malaya Neva River; when
discovered, the hands imply Rasputin was not dead when he was
thrown in, starting a legend of a devil with superhuman strength

**The Romanovs were murdered by
revolutionaries in 1918**

SPANISH FLU

In 1918 a world already devastated by war was shattered by the deaths of tens of millions of people from a terrifying superbug, nicknamed Spanish Flu.

 DATE 1918–19

DISEASE INFLUENZA A (H1N1)

SYMPTOMS FEVER, HEADACHES, FATIGUE, OFTEN LED TO PNEUMONIA

 ESTIMATED DEATHS 25–50 MILLION WORLDWIDE

 REGIONS AFFECTED NEARLY EVERYWHERE, SAVE FOR A FEW REMOTE ISLANDS

The disease's "first wave" devastated military hospitals around Europe. **Returning soldiers brought the virus home for second and third waves**, where most victims were young, healthy adults.

TREATMENT

No one knew about viruses, so **there was no vaccine and no cure**. Isolation, quarantine, closure of public buildings, and personal hygiene were the best solutions the authorities could offer.

675,000
Number of deaths
in the U.S.

New York City fined or even **jailed people who did not cover their coughs**.

WHY "SPANISH" FLU?

Due to the need **to keep up morale**, governments **kept the severity of the disease quiet during the war**. Spain, which was neutral, had freely reported it, receiving the dubious honor of being associated with the virus.

RECURRING NIGHTMARE

Spanish Flu **continued to reappear** as a seasonal disease across the globe **for the next thirty-eight years**.

In 2005 researchers at America's Centers for Disease Control **successfully reconstructed the H1N1 virus in order to study pandemic control**.

RUSSIAN REVOLUTIONS

*Turbulent times in the early twentieth century saw a series of revolutions,
gradually leading to the declaration of the Soviet Union.*

TIMELINE

Dates are given according to the Gregorian calendar, adopted by Soviet Russia in 1918

WAR YEARS

1861 Serfdom ends but Russian peasants are still tied to the land

1881 Czar Alexander II is assassinated by radical group People's Will

1882 Violent pogroms lead to mass Jewish migration

1894 Nicholas II ascends the throne

1905 "Bloody Sunday" begins the 1905 Revolution

1905 Sailors mutiny on Battleship *Potemkin*

1905 Nicholas issues the October Manifesto, promising civil liberties

1907 A coup ends in the dissolution of the Imperial Duma of the Russian legislative assembly

1914 Outbreak of the First World War

VLADIMIR LENIN

(1870–1924)
Revolutionary radical and eventual **leader of Soviet Russia**, Lenin was imprisoned for his views but came to prominence during the Bolshevik uprisings.

BLOODY SUNDAY

Police and soldiers open fire on a **peaceful demonstration, killing 1,000**. Czar Nicholas II was blamed.

THE FEBRUARY REVOLUTION

Eight days of public protests, beginning with a march of women, resulted in the abolition of the Russian monarchy. **Nicholas abdicated on March 15** but unrest against the new provisional government led to a wavering of power.

THE RED TERROR

A **period of mass arrests** and executions following an assassination attempt on Lenin.

1917 The February Revolution; on September 14 Russia is declared a republic

The October Revolution sees the Bolsheviks take control, declaring new workers' rights and the abolition of private property

1918 Bolshevik Russia loses much of the old empire as it quits the First World War

The Russian royal family are executed

The Red Terror begins

1922 The Soviet Union is created

1924 Lenin dies; a power struggle between Leon Trotsky and Joseph Stalin is eventually won by Stalin

1,300 PEOPLE KILLED

in the **Khodynka Tragedy,** a stampede at Nicholas II's coronation, on **May 30, 1896**

BAUHAUS

Originated in 1919, the Staatliches Bauhaus school of design, architecture and applied arts created work so timeless it still looks modern today.

STAATLICHES BAUHAUS

 DATES 1919–33

 CLOSED 1933 DUE TO PRESSURE FROM THE NAZIS

 LOCATIONS WEIMAR, 1919–25, DESSAU 1925–32, BERLIN 1932–33

 LOCATION NEW BAUHAUS OPENED IN CHICAGO 1937

 FOUNDED WALTER GROPIUS (1883–1969)

Gropius combined two schools, the Weimar Academy of Arts and the Weimar School of Arts and Crafts, into one **Bauhaus "house of building."**

ETHOS

While acknowledging the British Arts and Crafts movement, which combined craft and design, Gropius eschewed individually crafted luxury items in favor of **high-quality mass production**. He wanted to create aesthetically **pleasing items for every section of society**.

STUDENTS LEARNED BOTH THEORY AND PRACTICE IN:

- Carpentry
- Metalwork
- Pottery
- Stained glass
- Mural
- Weaving
- Graphics
- Typography
- Stagecraft

Graduates were equally at home with modern architecture and interior design.

THE TUBULAR CHAIR

Bauhaus students were **encouraged to use modern materials such as steel tubing, plywood, glass slabs, and geometric forms** to create beautiful, functional buildings and furniture.

Perhaps the most famous is Marcel Breuer's B3 chair, later named the **Wassily chair**, constructed from tubular steel and strips of black leather.

INFLUENCE

Bauhaus teaching methods and respect for design in everyday objects remain a strong part of many design curriculums today.

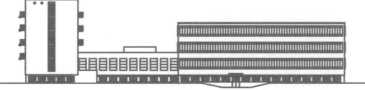

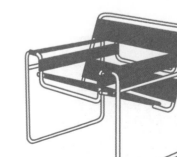

THE DISCOVERY OF THE TOMB OF TUTANKHAMUN

"Yes, wonderful things!" On being asked if he could see anything, archaeologist Howard Carter's reply is one of history's great understatements. The contents of boy-king Tutankhamun's undisturbed tomb remain the world's greatest archaeological find.

 LOCATION THE VALLEY OF THE KINGS, EGYPT

DATES

- **1323 BC** Tutankhamun dies, aged about eighteen; he is embalmed and laid to rest with everything he needs for the afterlife

- **1907** Lord Carnarvon hires Howard Carter to excavate ancient Egyptian sites

- **November 4, 1922** A local water-fetcher discovers a stone step

- **November 26, 1922** Carter breaks the tomb's seal

- **February 16, 1923** The Pharaoh's sarcophagus is found intact

WAR YEARS

ONE LAST JOB

Carter was originally hired by Carnarvon in 1907. After a series of setbacks, including the First World War, Carnarvon was disenchanted by the lack of results. But **Carter persuaded his sponsor to fund one last season**.

TREASURE

More than **3,000 ARTIFACTS** including priceless gold furniture, wall paintings, chariots, wine flasks, and even bread rolls were discovered. **Many are now on display in the Egyptian Museum in Cairo.**

COURT MASK

Tutankhamun's solid-gold death mask, **inlaid with enamel and semiprecious stones**, has a spell from the Ancient Egyptian Book of the Dead engraved on the back.

TUT FEVER

The world was captivated by the discovery and **ancient Egyptian style became "modern," finding its way into fashion, architecture, and design**, and was epitomized in the new Art Deco style.

ALBERT EINSTEIN

Geniuses rarely come more popular than Albert Einstein, lauded for his contributions to science, loved for his sense of fun and commitment to peace.

 BORN MARCH 14, 1879, ULM, GERMANY

DIED APRIL 18, 1955, PRINCETON, UNITED STATES

Einstein hated school. His head teacher announced he would never make a success of anything.

He finally took a job as an **admin officer at the Swiss Patent Office**. His work wasn't arduous and allowed him time to think. He began working on his own.

ANNUS MIRABILIS

In 1905 26-year-old Einstein published four papers. He:

- **Proved atoms exist**, winning a PhD
- Started the concept of **Quantum Mechanics**
- Came up with the **Special Theory of Relativity**
- **Introduced the equation E=MC²**, theorizing that matter and energy are interchangeable

EINSTEIN'S THEORIES OF RELATIVITY

The Special Theory of Relativity proposes **speed always relates to something else** and how fast the other object is going.

The General Theory of Relativity is a **theory of gravity**. It describes the fabric of space and time and how this can be bent, stretched, distorted, and perhaps even broken.

PACIFIST

The First World War was distressing for Einstein, **a committed pacifist**. As a Jew he was made uncomfortable when he tried to return to Nazi Germany. **He moved countries, eventually settling in Princeton, United States**. His work led to the **Manhattan Project** but he worked tirelessly to prevent the proliferation of nuclear weapons.

WAR YEARS

LADIES' MAN

Einstein was popular with women and he had a turbulent personal life, marrying his first cousin after settling his first divorce with his Nobel Prize money.

PROHIBITION

America had always had its hard drinkers—Civil War soldiers used to sneak bottles of booze into camp inside their trousers, earning the name "bootleggers." As life settled down, however, teetotallers began to believe alcohol was the root of America's problems.

START

JANUARY 16, 1919
The Eighteenth Amendment to the Constitution outlaws all production, imports, sales, and transport of alcohol.

END

DECEMBER 5,1933
The Twenty-First Amendment to the Constitution ends prohibition.

THE NOBLE EXPERIMENT

Prohibitionists claimed alcohol caused crime, family breakups, health problems, and was against the will of God. In the early twentieth century members of the temperance movement started to call for it to be banned.

UNFORESEEN CONSEQUENCES

Prohibition opened up a **massive black market in smuggled alcohol, speakeasies, and criminal activity**. A new breed of racketeer started importing or manufacturing hooch, at first clandestinely, then openly, with corrupt city officials turning a blind eye. **Gangland violence reached dizzying new heights** and revenue from alcohol taxes nosedived.

Homemade "moonshine" could be a killer and industrial alcohol, deliberately contaminated, was often resold for drinking.

Enforcement was almost impossible due to America's large borders, bribery of officials, and public noncooperation.

PROHIBITION IN NUMBERS

32,000
Speakeasies in New York in 1929

280,000
Illegal stills seized in 1929

130
Gangland murders in Chicago between 1926 and 1927

ALCOHOL-RELATED DEATHS

1926	1920
760	**98**

BENITO MUSSOLINI

Son of a blacksmith, Benito Mussolini began his political life as a socialist. He would become one of the most notorious fascist leaders of the twentieth century.

TIMELINE

- **July 29, 1883** Born in Predappio, Italy

- **1902** Moves to Switzerland to find work; joins socialist newspaper *Avanti*

- **1915** Disenchanted with socialism, joins the army on Italy's entry into the First World War

- **1919** Forms the Fascist Party

- **1921** The Fascist Party joins Italy's coalition government

- **1922** Mussolini's Black Shirts march on Rome and King Victor Emmanuel invites him to form a government

- **1925** Now dictator, declares himself Il Duce, "the leader"

- **1935** Invades Abyssinia (now Ethiopia) and supports General Francisco Franco in the Spanish Civil War

- **1939** Signs the Pact of Steel military alliance with Nazi Germany; introduces anti-Jewish legislation

- **1940** Italy declares war on Britain and France but is defeated in North and East Africa and the Balkans

- **1943** Mussolini overthrown and imprisoned by former government colleagues; Italy is occupied by the Nazis, with Mussolini reinstated as a puppet leader

- **1945** Flees from Allied troops but is captured and shot on April 28

CULT OF PERSONALITY

Mussolini had a charisma and manner of public speaking **that inspired devotion** even when his government was not strong.

THE BLACK SHIRTS

Mussolini harnessed the discontent of unemployed war veterans into armed terrorist squads, which intimidated their political opponents. **Their motto was "*Me ne frego*"— "I don't give a damn."**

ITALY UNDER MUSSOLINI

The state controlled every aspect of life, backed up by OVRA, the secret police. Youth organizations nurtured junior fascists as bold male soldiers and strong female mothers.

5	**IN 1940**
The number of children women were to aim for, under **Mussolini's Battle for Births initiative**	**4,000** People sent to prison by OVRA
	10 Sentenced to death

TALKING PICTURES

Giving silent movies voice was the biggest revolution cinema has ever undergone. With the success of The Jazz Singer, *all bets were off.*

THE "SILENT" ERA

In the silent movie era, films were accompanied with live music, usually piano. Intertitles conveyed the most important parts, and actors used exaggerated gestures and expressions to show emotion.

TIMELINE

WAR YEARS

1877 Thomas Edison invents the phonograph; he tries to combine sound and early moving pictures

1900 The Phono-Cinema in Paris plays phonographs with moving pictures, cranking the sound faster to keep up with events onscreen

1913 Léon Gaumont invents a mechanical amplifier

1919 Lee De Forest photographically records sound onto the side of film strips

1920s Silent movies are all the rage; Hollywood is not keen on changing to new tech

1927 *The Jazz Singer* is the first commercial sound hit

THE PROBLEMS

Dozens of inventors wrestled with bringing sound to the cinema. They needed to synchronize sound so it came from the actors' lips as they spoke, then make it loud enough to hear.

Silent audiences had learned the "shorthand" of silent films and **needed a lot of persuasion to adopt the new-fangled "talkies."**

PRODUCTION HELL

Sound recording was noisy and fraught with problems, as famously lampooned in the 1952 Hollywood musical *Singin' in the Rain.*

Some famous actors didn't sound right and lost their jobs almost overnight. **International audiences could no longer just switch language on the intertitles, and the old scripts seemed overplayed.** But once the public heard Al Jolson sing, there was no going back.

PRODUCTION HEAVEN

Sound meant drama could be deeper and comedy could be vocal as well as visual. **The Hollywood musical was born.**

As the Great Depression loomed, at least one thing was gorgeous: cinema.

AL CAPONE

Probably the most notorious gangster of all time, Alphonse Gabriel Capone was a black-hearted villain to some, a hero to others.

 DATES BORN JANUARY 17, 1899; DIED JANUARY 25, 1947

 NICKNAMES AL, SNORKY, SCARFACE

 RACKET BOOTLEGGING

 **SIDELINES** SPEAKEASIES, DOG TRACKS, CASINOS, NIGHTCLUBS, EXTORTION, MURDER, JURY HARASSMENT, POLICE BRIBERY, ELECTION RIGGING

PROFITS UNKNOWN; CAPONE DIDN'T HAVE A BANK ACCOUNT

Born in Brooklyn, New York, **Capone found his metier in Chicago, where he became a boss of organized crime**. Prohibition had created an opening for illegal liquor and he was determined to fill it, regardless of the violence the job might require.

ST. VALENTINE'S DAY MASSACRE

On **February 14, 1929**, a group of "policemen" raided the garage where Capone's rival, Bugs Moran, was meeting his gang. **Seven gang members were shot. Bugs swore it was Capone.**

THE UNTOUCHABLES

Prohibition agent Eliot Ness put together **a group of police that were "incorruptible,"** and declared war on Scarface. They made headlines with every raid, but **they couldn't pin anything on Capone**. Frank Wilson, of the Internal Revenue Service, finally managed to make a charge stick—tax evasion.

SENTENCE

Capone spent **eleven years in jail**, several of which were in the newly built Alcatraz Federal Penitentiary.

FOLK HERO

Al Capone was known to help "the little people," arranging a soup kitchen for down-and-outs and paying the hospital bill of a passerby who'd been shot by a bullet meant for him.

THE WEIMAR REPUBLIC

On the abdication of the German Kaiser at the end of the First World War, Germany was both defeated and broken.

TIMELINE

November 11, 1918
Germany surrenders

January 1919 Friedrich Ebert becomes president of the Social Democratic Party, which meets temporarily in the town of Weimar

July 1919 The Treaty of Versailles punishes Germany—financially, militarily, and emotionally

1923 Germany faces hyperinflation

1924 Weimar Germany stabilizes

1929 The Great Depression leads to deprivation, desperation, and the rise of national socialism

WAR YEARS

NOVEMBER CRIMINALS

The men who signed the Treaty of Versailles were regarded by many as traitors to Germany.

HYPERINFLATION

Instability meant **the weak Weimar government had to print money**, leading to hyperinflation. Workers had to be **paid twice a day to keep up**, and they went shopping with **wheelbarrows full of cash**.

ARTICLE 48

The constitution allowed the President to override Parliament in an "emergency," but the provision was badly overused

ART

In spite of political turmoil, **Weimar Germany saw a golden age in art and architecture**. The **Bauhaus** school brought a new architectural style to the world. The iconoclastic **Dada movement influenced art, while expressionism seeped a new darkness into German cinema**. In Berlin, a hedonistic, devil-take-tomorrow cabaret culture partied in the face of the rise of **the darkest movement of all: Nazism**.

COST OF A LOAF OF BREAD
January 1923 = **250 MARKS**

November 1923 = **200,000 MILLION MARKS**

THE GREAT DEPRESSION

On October 29, 1929, the Roaring Twenties crashed. The U.S. stock market went into freefall, banks failed, fortunes were lost, and, over the months and years that followed, millions starved.

BUILD-UP

In the 1920s the U.S. was booming. Ordinary Americans found employment easily, **Henry Ford's cars were selling fast**, and, for some, borrowing money to play the stock market became all the rage.

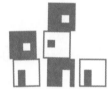

OCTOBER 1929

18th Stock market prices begin to fall
24th Black Thursday: bankers start buying shares to stabilize the market
29th Black Tuesday: the Wall Street crash; share prices collapse

Wealthy people went bankrupt overnight. It didn't take long for regular people to be pushed into poverty. **Thousands lost their homes, living in shanty towns called Hoovervilles, after President Hoover**, who many felt did not care about their plight.

Soup kitchens became common. In Chicago in 1930, gangster Al Capone provided a Thanksgiving beef stew for 5,000 hungry people.

DUST BOWL

The Great Plains had been eroded by overfarming, turning once-fertile soil to dust. Many abandoned everything and joined the throngs driving, hitching, or walking to California, where things would be better—or at least Hollywood told them so.

FDR

In the 1933 presidential election Hoover was beaten by Franklin D. Roosevelt, who promised a New Deal.

NEW DEAL

Roosevelt created jobs for the unemployed on grand programs of renewal through clearing, renovation, and construction. His regular radio "fireside chats" helped to calm the situation, but plenty was not enjoyed again until after the Second World War.

ADOLF HITLER

Of the many horrific dictators thrown up by the twentieth century, the name of Adolf Hitler is perhaps the most reviled. Somewhere along the line a failed artist became a very successful mass murderer.

TIMELINE

- **April 20, 1889** Born in Braunau am Inn, Austria

- **1903** Rejected by Vienna Academy of Fine Arts

- **1914** Enthusiastically joins the German Army in the First World War

- **1918** Disgusted at Germany's surrender and the Weimar government, joins the nationalist, anti-Semitic German Workers' Party

- **1921** Charismatic speeches gain him sole control of the party

- **1923** After bursting into a beer hall with storm troopers, he is sentenced to five years in prison; he serves nine months

- **1925** *Mein Kampf* is published

- **1933** Becomes Chancellor of Germany

- **1934** Hundreds of political rivals assassinated by the SS in the Night of the Long Knives, affording him total control

- **1935** Passes the Nuremberg Laws, denying rights to Jewish and other "undesirable" people

- **1938** Begins territorial expansion

- **1939** Nazi invasion of Poland, followed by much of Europe

- **1945** Soviet troops invade Berlin. Hitler marries his lover Eva Braun, before the couple commit suicide with cyanide on April 30

WAR YEARS

ORIGINS OF HATE

While living in Vienna, **Hitler was inspired by the anti-Semitic policies of the city's mayor, Karl Lueger**.

MOUSTACHE

Convalescing from injuries sustained at the Battle of the Somme, Hitler began wearing his trademark moustache.

SWASTIKA

This ancient Indian symbol, meaning "well-being," was a popular good luck symbol in the West until it **was hijacked by the Nazis**.

MEIN KAMPF

Hitler's manifesto was a blast of **anti-Semitic, nationalist bile** advocating military expansion, the elimination of "impure" races, and dictatorship. It was a huge hit.

SS

The "Schutzstaffel" was a **paramilitary force Hitler used to reign by terror**.

VOTES FOR THE NAZI PARTY

2.6% 1928 elections
37% 1932 elections

FRANKLIN D. ROOSEVELT

Franklin Delano Roosevelt came to power in troubled times. Both admired and hated, he guided America through the Depression and World War II with his steady hand and "fireside chats."

TIMELINE

- **January 30, 1882** Born in Hyde Park, New York

- **1900** Enters Harvard University

- **1905** Marries his distant cousin, Eleanor Roosevelt

- **1910** Wins an "unwinnable" seat in the New York State Senate for the Democrats

- **1913** Appointed Secretary of the Navy

- **1914–18** Admired as an effective naval administrator in the First World War

- **1921** Contracts polio, losing the use of his legs

- **1928** Becomes Governor of New York, winning again in 1930

- **1931** Creates the Temporary Emergency Relief Administration

- **1932** Becomes 32nd President of the United States in a landslide victory; begins the New Deal

- **1935** The second New Deal

- **1936** Reelected President

- **1940** Reelected President for a third term

- **1941** Attack on Pearl Harbor brings America into the Second World War

- **1944** Wins a fourth term as President

- **April 12, 1945** Dies in Warm Springs, Georgia

THE NEW DEAL

Roosevelt's admittedly **experimental series of work-creation programs and financial reforms** were designed to help ordinary Americans through the Great Depression. He was **assisted by advisors known as The Brains Trust**. The program's vast construction works included buildings, roads, bridges, and airports as well as conservation and cultural projects.

PUBLIC UTILITIES

Building hydroelectric dams gave work to thousands and provided cheap electricity to even more. Other work-creation schemes involved reforestation and flood control.

WIRELESS

Roosevelt's mastery of radio in his famous "fireside chats" steadied the nation, helping them feel that he was in control.

5	4
Franklin D. was fifth **cousin to Theodore Roosevelt**, 26th President	**terms as President**, and the only one to be elected to serve more than two
13 MILLION **unemployed** when Roosevelt took office	**2.1 MILLION** Monthly average number of **New Deal workers 1935–41**

THE SPANISH CIVIL WAR

Starting as a military revolt, the Spanish Civil War became one of the bloodiest in history.

 DATES JULY 18, 1936–APRIL 1, 1939

 LOCATION SPAIN

 COMBATANTS THE SPANISH REPUBLIC VS NATIONALIST REBELS

 DEATHS THE NUMBER CAN ONLY BE ROUGHLY ESTIMATED, BUT COULD BE UP TO 1 MILLION

 RESULT NATIONALIST DICTATORSHIP UNDER FRANCO

WAR YEARS

TIMELINE

1936

February A coalition of left-wing parties narrowly wins Spain's general election

July After a military coup led by General Francisco Franco, Nationalist rebels begin taking over Spain

October Madrid is put under siege by the Nationalists

1937

March 8–27 Republicans force the Nationalists into retreat at Guadalajara but Madrid still threatened

April 26 Franco bombs Guernica, killing thousands; his forces take Malaga but the Republic forces him back from Madrid

1938

March 16–18 Barcelona is heavily bombed

1939

March 28 Franco marches into Madrid

April 1 Franco proclaims victory

BACKGROUND

The Great Depression hit Spain badly. **Its starving, unemployed people could not agree who was to blame.**

The Republicans were fragmented, ranging from moderate to anarchist. **The Nationalists appealed to a general sense of fear of communism**, calling Republicans "reds," a threat to the establishment and the Christian faith.

NATIONALISTS

were often supported by:
- Landowners
- Businessmen
- The military
- The Catholic Church

REPUBLICANS

were more diverse, comprising:
- Foreign volunteers
- Urban workers
- Laborers
- The middle class

NAZI TROOPS

Hitler and Mussolini sent financial and military aid to the Nationalist rebels. The USSR sent some support to the Republicans.

EL CAUDILLO

Rebel turned military dictator General Francisco Franco styled himself "The Chief."

THE 1936 OLYMPIC GAMES

1936 marked the first time in the history of the modern Olympic Games that people called for a boycott due to human rights abuses. After promising not to use the Games for propaganda, Adolf Hitler did precisely that.

 DATES AUGUST 1–16, 1936

LOCATION BERLIN

 COUNTRIES ATTENDING 49

 ATHLETES ATTENDING 4,000

 EVENTS 129

Germany was granted the Olympics in 1931, **two years before Hitler came to power**.

"ARYAN PERFECTION"

Nazi propaganda promoted the myth of "Aryan" superiority, idealizing the physical stature of people with features recognized as of the "correct" race.

SEEDS OF DISCONTENT

In April 1933 all German athletic organizations included an Aryan-only policy, barring people of Jewish or Roma descent. **Champions that did not fit the Nazi ideal were removed from the team.**

BOYCOTT

Calls for boycott came from around the world. **After agreeing to tone down the propaganda and field Jewish competitors, Hitler was allowed to proceed.**

Pressured into sending **Jewish athletes, the German team sent just one—fencer Helene Mayer**. She was expected to give the Nazi salute, like all the other German winners.

THE PEOPLE'S OLYMPIAD

An alternative Olympics, supported by many boycotting the official Games, **was to be held in Barcelona**. It was canceled at the outbreak of the Spanish Civil War.

JESSE OWENS

The most successful athlete at the games, **African American Jesse Owens, proved Hitler wrong**. He was the first American to win four track and field gold medals at a single Olympics.

OLYMPIA

In 1938 filmmaker **Leni Riefenstahl** released this documentary as **propaganda for the Nazi regime**.

Germany invaded Poland on September 1, 1939, three years after showing a hospitable and peaceful face at the Olympic Games.

THE 1936 OLYMPIC GAMES IN NUMBERS

800 Roma were arrested in Berlin, on July 16, 1936, and interned in the suburb of Marzahn

9 Jewish athletes won medals

348 athletes came from Nazi Germany

312 athletes came from the U.S., including 18 African Americans

THE HINDENBURG DISASTER

At 7:25 p.m. on May 6, 1937, the Hindenburg *airship burst into flames while attempting to land at Lakehurst, New Jersey.*

 THE LZ 129 HINDENBURG LARGEST RIGID AIRSHIP EVER CONSTRUCTED

 DESIGN ZEPPELIN STYLE

 LAUNCHED FRIEDRICHSHAFEN, GERMANY, MARCH 1936

 MAX SPEED 78 MPH

 CAUSE OF FIRE ATMOSPHERIC ELECTRICITY AND A HYDROGEN GAS LEAK

ONBOARD FACILITIES

- 72 passenger beds in heated cabins
- Dining room
- Lounge
- Writing room
- Bar
- Smoking room
- Promenades

The ship was designed to be filled with the inert gas helium but was instead inflated with highly flammable hydrogen.

The *Hindenburg* had previously made **many successful trips**, carrying thousands of passengers between Germany and the U.S..

On August 1, 1936, the *Hindenburg* flew over the Olympic stadium in Berlin.

NAZI PROPAGANDA

The ship also **made an appearance at the Nuremberg Rally**, and its livery included a swastika.

THE RADIO ANNOUNCER

WLS Radio presenter **Herb Morrison was broadcasting the landing in New Jersey live to tens of thousands**. His horrified "Oh, the humanity!" summed up feelings across the world.

$450 Price of a one-way ticket on the *Hindenburg* in 1937 ($7,800 or £6,000 today).

The *Hindenburg* disaster marked the end of dirigibles as a form of commercial transportation.

THE HINDENBURG IN NUMBERS

- 22 crew
- 13 passengers
- 1 ground crew

61 survivors

97 persons on board
36 people killed

C.200 FT. Height off the ground when it combusted; as it fell, many jumped

12 HOURS Delay caused by strong winds and a wait for storms to clear

4 newsreel companies filmed the first disaster caught on camera

34 SECONDS Time it took for the *Hindenburg* to burn

WORLD WAR II

Few nations remained neutral in the devastating conflict of 1939–45. On one side were the Axis powers behind Germany, Italy, and Japan; on the other the Allied nations including Great Britain, France, and the United States.

 DATES SEPTEMBER 3, 1939–AUGUST 15, 1945

 LOCATION WORLDWIDE

 COMBATANTS AXIS NATIONS VS ALLIED NATIONS

 CASUALTIES ESTIMATES VARY BETWEEN 50 MILLION AND 80 MILLION

 RESULT VICTORY FOR THE ALLIED NATIONS

TIMELINE

- **September 1, 1939** Adolf Hitler invades Poland; Britain and France declare war on Germany on September 3

- **1940** Germany invades Belgium, Holland, and France in the Blitzkrieg; Allied forces rescued from Dunkirk

- **1941** Hitler aims to invade Russia and continues to bomb UK cities; Japan attacks Pearl Harbor, bringing the U.S. into the war

- **1942** Japan takes Singapore, seizing about 25,000 prisoners; mass murder begins in Auschwitz and other concentration camps

- **1943** Germany's first major defeat at Stalingrad; Italy is invaded by the Allies, Germany continues the fight, and Britain and India fight the Japanese in Burma

- **1944** D-Day brings the Allied invasion of France; Paris is liberated; Guam is liberated by the U.S.

- **1945** Auschwitz is liberated. Soviet troops enter Berlin; Hitler commits suicide; Germany surrenders on May 7. The U.S. drops atomic bombs on Hiroshima and Nagasaki; Japan surrenders August 14

THE PHONEY WAR

After the declaration of war in 1939, Europe went quiet as both sides equipped themselves.

BLITZKRIEG

The **"lightning war" involved the heavy bombing of western European cities.** The Allies responded in kind, aerial-bombing German cities including Berlin and Dresden.

PROPAGANDA

All sides used propaganda during the war, ranging from leaflet drops to posters. Charismatic leaders such as **Hitler, Winston Churchill, and Franklin D. Roosevelt used modern media such as newsreels and radio broadcasts** to keep up morale—and demoralize the other side.

DEATHS BY AIR RAID

Germany: **543,000** Britain: **60,400**
Military deaths: **WWI 95%, WWII 5%**
Civilian deaths: **WWI 33%, WWII 67%**

AXIS V ALLIED

Countries supporting Germany, Japan, and Italy were pitched against over fifty Allied Nations including the United States, Great Britain, France, and the Soviet Union.

CRACKING THE ENIGMA CODE

One of World War II's deadliest hazards was the German targeting of merchant ships delivering supplies to Britain. Until their secret code was broken, the U-boats could not be intercepted.

 NAME THE GOVERNMENT CODE AND CYPHER SCHOOL

 MISSION TO CRACK THE ENIGMA CODE

 LOCATION BLETCHLEY PARK, NEAR MILTON KEYNES, UK

 DATES 1939–46

BREAKTHROUGH

On May 9, 1941, **codebooks and an Enigma machine were seized from captured German U-boat U-110**.

Thousands worked in Bletchley's city of wooden huts but no one knew what anyone else did. Unable to talk about work, **social events were wide and varied**.

HUT EIGHT

A small group, including mathematician **Alan Turing, invented an electro-mechanical machine called a "bombe,"** which could cycle through possible common words in a message more quickly than humans.

WHAT WAS THE ENIGMA MACHINE?

Enigma was an **automated message scrambler invented in the 1920s**. As a message was typed, **Enigma covered it with multiple layers of ever-changing encryption, to be sent safely by Morse code**. The code was changed every day at midnight.

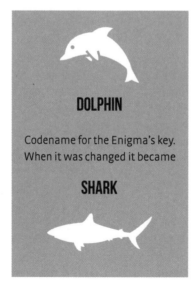

DOLPHIN

Codename for the Enigma's key. When it was changed it became

SHARK

COLOSSUS The world's first practical digital information **processing computer was built by Tommy Flowers in 1944**.

10,000
Number of workers at Bletchley in 1945, **mainly women**

THE EVACUATION OF DUNKIRK

A massive propaganda coup, the brave "little ships" that rescued the stranded Allies from the beaches of Dunkirk in May 1940 paid a high price for their place in history.

OPERATION DYNAMO IN NUMBERS

8,000
Soldiers rescued
on the first day

338,226
Troops saved overall

140,000
French, Polish, and Belgian
troops saved

BACKGROUND

Forced to retreat to the town of Dunkirk in northern France, **the British Expeditionary Forces did not really expect to be rescued any more than their superiors expected to rescue them**.

Operation Dynamo was a long shot. Vice-Admiral Bertram Ramsay had to gather together a flotilla of destroyers, supplemented by whatever else could be mustered.

While some units fought the Germans on land and the RAF battled the Luftwaffe in the sky, troops queued as though for buses. **Many left from a jetty known as the Dunkirk Mole.**

Over the next week, **thousands were rescued**, some ships making many hazardous trips, **loaded to capacity and under a constant rain of German bombs**.

A LIMITED SUCCESS

More than **236 vessels and thousands of men never made it home**, including the troopship *Lancastria*, **sunk with a loss of 3,500 lives**.

Nearly **140,000 British troops remained in France**, captured or forced to surrender and taken to prisoner of war camps. **On June 4 Dunkirk fell to the Nazi army.**

"Dunkirk spirit" is still a byword for facing adversity.

On **Sunday, May 26 the first of 933 craft left Ramsgate in Kent**, including:
- Ferries
- Paddle steamers
- Coasters
- Motor launches
- Tugboats
- Pleasure craft
- Flat-bottomed Dutch barges
- Fishing boats
- Lifeboats
- Private yachts

Many were piloted by their civilian owners.

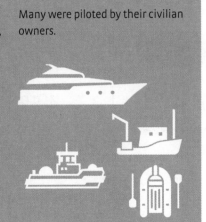

THE ATTACK ON PEARL HARBOR

A surprise, two-hour aerial raid on a U.S. naval base on a remote island in the South Pacific Ocean turned a multinational conflict into a world war.

 DATE SUNDAY, DECEMBER 7, 1941

 LOCATION OAHU, HAWAII

 COMBATANTS JAPAN VS UNITED STATES

 CASUALTIES AMERICA: NEARLY 2,500 KILLED, 1,000 WOUNDED; JAPAN: 64 KILLED, 1 TAKEN PRISONER

 RESULT AMERICA JOINS WORLD WAR II

BACKGROUND

Japan and the U.S. had felt **mutual aggression for years**. America, fearful of Japan's expansion into China, had imposed heavy sanctions.

Japan wanted to intimidate the U.S. and neutralize a fleet that might hinder its position in the South Pacific.

THE ATTACK

At 07:55 Pearl Harbor fell into the shadow of 353 Japanese fighter planes. Bombs rained down on the relatively lightly defended base.

At 08:10 a bomb hit USS *Arizona*, smashing through the deck into the ammunition store.

The ship exploded and sank, taking 1,177 men with it.

At 08:54 a second attack began.

After two hours, every ship on base was badly damaged or sunk.

SMALL CONSOLATION

Luckily for the U.S., **the fleet's aircraft carriers were away from base**.

AMERICAN SHOCK AND FURY

On **December 8, 1941, President Franklin D. Roosevelt**, widely supported by an outraged American public, **asked Congress to declare war on Japan**.

On **December 11 Japan's allies, Italy and Germany, declared war on the United States**. World War II began in earnest.

GLENN MILLER: THE SOUND OF WORLD WAR II

As the bombs fell in war-torn Europe, wirelesses and picture houses brought American-style music to the stuffy, rationed world of 1940s Britain. Major Glenn Miller's big band was the biggest of them all.

 BORN IOWA, 1904

 INSTRUMENT TROMBONE

 FIRST BIG BAND 1937

 DEATH MISSING IN ACTION, 1944

BACKGROUND

Jazz music came of age in the 1930s, with bandleaders such as **Benny Goodman**, **Tommy Dorsey**, **Artie Shaw**, **Count Basie**, and **Duke Ellington** ruling the roost.

Britain had its own popular dance orchestras but **Hollywood turned American big bands into superstars**.

DOIN' THE JIVE

The new dance craze brought over by the GIs shocked and excited Brits in equal measure. Crazy "jitterbug" moves were fast, furious—and sexy.

THE SOUND

Miller's unique sound involved tenor saxophones and clarinets playing the melody together, while lush trombones "talked" in the background.

U.S. ARMY

In **1942 Miller enlisted in the U.S. Army and was assigned to the Air Force Band**. He boosted troop morale by cleverly combining the big band blues sound with march time.

MOVIE STAR

The band starred in two Hollywood films, *Sun Valley Serenade* (1941) and *Orchestra Wives* (1942). They also made dozens of short "soundies," often including vocal group The Andrews Sisters.

TRAGEDY

Miller's mysterious **disappearance during a flight from England to Paris**, France, in 1944 only fueled his fame. His band continued to sell millions of records.

In 1954 James Stewart starred in *The Glenn Miller Story*, loosely based on the bandleader's life.

MILLER'S BIGGEST WARTIME HITS

- "Moonlight Serenade"
- "Chattanooga Choo-Choo"
- "In the Mood"
- "American Patrol"
- "Pennsylvania 6-5000"
- "Tuxedo Junction"
- "A String of Pearls"
- "St. Louis Blues March"

THE D-DAY LANDINGS

Months of top-secret planning culminated in 1944 when Operation Overlord kickstarted the final stages of World War II.

 DATE JUNE 6, 1944

 LOCATION NORMANDY BEACHES, FRANCE

 SUPREME ALLIED COMMANDER GENERAL DWIGHT D. EISENHOWER

 ALLIED GROUND FORCES COMMANDER FIELD MARSHAL BERNARD LAW MONTGOMERY

WAR YEARS

TIMELINE

00:00 Operation Titanic drops hundreds of dummy parachutists, distracting the enemy

00:10 First genuine paratroopers jump

01:20 Naval assault begins

02:00 First wave of bombers leaves Britain

02:51 U.S. ships begin to drop anchor

04:00 Sainte-Mère-Église is the first town liberated

05:30 Allies begin bombarding beaches

06:00 The BBC broadcasts a message to the people of Normandy, warning them to take shelter

BACKGROUND

By 1943 both sides knew an Allied invasion was on its way but **just a few individuals knew when**, where, and how.

OPERATION FORTITUDE

Government misinformation, fake planes and spoof artillery led the enemy into thinking the invasion would happen either on a **different part of the French coast or in Norway**.

THE BEACHES

Ground troops landed across five assault beaches, codenamed **Utah**, **Omaha**, **Gold**, **Juno**, and **Sword**, and established themselves as an invading force.

GUSTAV

An RAF pigeon used to send news during radio silence later received the Dickin Medal.

06:40 German resistance steps up

08:20 Relief troops from 1st Special Service Brigade march ashore; Piper Bill Millin plays "Highland Laddie"

09:05 Adolf Hitler still believes the real invasion is elsewhere

12:07 Winston Churchill addresses the House of Commons

13:00 The news is officially broadcast by the BBC

21:00 King George VI addresses the Empire

23:59 159,000 Allied services have established an invasion base; Europe waits to be liberated

THE LIBERATION OF AUSCHWITZ

As Soviet troops entered Auschwitz, the largest concentration camp built by the Nazis, the horrors they encountered were like nothing ever seen before.

 DATE JANUARY 27, 1945

 LOCATION AUSCHWITZ, 37 MILES WEST OF KRAKOW, POLAND

 AUSCHWITZ CONCENTRATION CAMP, KILLING ZONE, AND FORCED-LABOR COMPLEX

 MOTTO *ARBEIT MACHT FREI,* "WORK BRINGS FREEDOM"

 AFTERMATH A STATE COMMISSION IS COMPILED TO REVEAL THE CAMP'S FULL HORROR

PRELIBERATION

Hearing the Soviet Army is approaching, the SS begin evacuating the camp. **They destroy the gas chambers and crematoria in an attempt to cover their tracks.**

Sixty thousand men, women, and children are forced to march toward Wodzislaw 30 miles away. More than 15,000 starve, die from exposure, or are shot for falling behind.

LIBERATION

The Red Army discovers nearly **3,000 starving, dead, and dying prisoners who were too sick to leave**. They are **mainly Jewish, but also include political and homosexual prisoners and members of the traveling community**.

ALSO FOUND BY THE TROOPS:

- 7 tons of human hair
- Human teeth, from which the gold fillings had been removed
- Thousands of children's clothes

SURVIVOR STORY

Jozef Paczynski was a Polish political prisoner at Auschwitz from June 1940; he was personal barber to camp commander, Rudolf Höss. He survived at the camp for more than four and a half years, was later freed by US soldiers, and lived to the age of ninety-five.

6,000	4 MILLION	1–1.5 MILLION
Number of people who could be murdered in the gas chambers every day	Estimated number of people sent to Auschwitz from 1940 to 1945	Estimated number of people murdered at the camp

VE DAY

Victory in Europe Day heralded the end of nearly six years of war that had devastated Europe. It sparked wild celebrations across the world.

 DATE MAY 8, 1945

TIMELINE

- **April 30** Adolf Hitler commits suicide

- **May 4** British Field Marshal Montgomery accepts the unconditional surrender of Germany in the Netherlands, northwest Germany, and Denmark

- **May 7** General Eisenhower accepts unconditional surrender from the rest of the German forces

- A BBC newsflash announces the following day will be a national vacation; newspaper presses are stopped to make way for special editions

- **May 8** Churchill addresses the nation at 3:00 p.m.; the royal family appears on the balcony eight times; royal princesses Elizabeth and Margaret sneak out into the crowd to celebrate

WAR YEARS

Hope had been in the air for some time, and British people had been on tenterhooks waiting for the moment they could finally relax.

PEAKING EARLY

Some started celebrating immediately, lighting bonfires, dancing, and partying in bars.

SUPPLIES

Prime Minister Winston Churchill arranged for extra beer supplies, and people could buy red, white, and blue bunting without ration coupons.

CELEBRATION

GREAT BRITAIN	**AMERICA**	**PARIS**
Thanksgiving services, parades, and, most famously, street parties were held. People danced in the street to gramophone records and barrel organs.	**VE Day was tempered by the recent death of President Roosevelt** but on the streets of New York, especially Times Square, the crowds danced madly.	Recently liberated, it was said there was no room left to move in the streets.

Due to time differences, New Zealand's VE Day was held on May 9.

REALITY

VE Day was not the end of World War II. The world would have to wait until **August 15, VJ Day, when Victory over Japan finally signaled peace.** Many had lost loved ones, and rationing in England would not end until 1954.

HIROSHIMA

At 08:16 local time on August 6, 1945, Enola Gay, *an American B-29 bomber, dropped the* Little Boy, *the world's first atom bomb.*

C.290,000
Civilians living in Hiroshima before the blast

20
Number of the city's 200 doctors able to work after the bomb

KOKURA & NAGASAKI
Back-up targets in case of fog

60,000–80,000
Japanese citizens killed instantly; thousands more died over the following months and years

BACKGROUND

Japan had been consistently bombed with conventional weapons, but was showing no signs of surrender. **President Harry S. Truman felt he faced two options: full-scale invasion under Operation Downfall, or the A-bomb.**

THE MANHATTAN PROJECT

The **fear that the Nazis were developing nuclear bombs spurred the U.S. government to begin their own research project**, exploiting nuclear fission for military purposes.

AFTERMATH

A victory parade carried Colonel Paul Tibbets and his crew through New York City but **it was only after the second bomb, dubbed "Fat Man," was dropped on Nagasaki that Japan finally surrendered.**

One building remained after the attack in Hiroshima, a domed exhibition building now designated as **the Peace Memorial**.

WHAT IT WAS LIKE

Eyewitnesses described a blinding flash, followed by a resounding boom. **The initial blast was so intense people were incinerated on the spot, leaving strange, ghostly silhouettes.** Many not killed by the blast died in hundreds of fires.

WHY HIROSHIMA?

The **traditional Japanese port was part of the country's supply chain**; it had also not been bombed yet. Truman needed somewhere "clean" that could demonstrate the devastation an atomic bomb was able to wreak.

THE COLD WAR

*Although they had fought together against a common enemy in World War II,
the United States and Soviet Union had very different political agendas.
Once the war was over, suspicion grew between the two nations.*

The Americans were suspicious of communism; they watched the bloodthirsty reign of the Soviet leader Joseph Stalin with horror and **feared Soviet expansion could destabilize the world**.

The Soviet Union was angry that the United States refused to include the USSR in the international community.

COLD WAR TO PRESENT DAY

TIMELINE

- **1947** President Harry Truman announces to U.S. Congress his intention to support "free peoples resisting subjugation"; in other words, to oppose communist expansion

- **1950–53** Korean War

- **1962** Cuban Missile Crisis

- **1972** President Nixon's policy of détente (release from tension) reduces the threat of nuclear war

- **1983** President Reagan's Strategic Defense Initiative, a.k.a. Star Wars, starts to heat the Cold War again

- **1985** Premier Mikhail Gorbachev's policies of *glasnost* (openness) and *perestroika* (economic reform) begin to signal change

- **1989** The fall of the Berlin Wall brings the end of the Cold War

The Cold War was particularly dangerous as both sides had the atomic bomb. As relations cooled, a nuclear arms race began.

THE H-BOMB

First tested in 1952 on the Enewetak Atoll, the H-bomb created a **25-square-mile fireball** that vaporized an island.

SURVIVAL

Fearful American citizens built fallout shelters in their back yards and stockpiled supplies, while their children practiced nuclear drills in school.

$100 MILLION allocated by Congress to build public bomb shelters

THE SPACE RACE

As space exploration became within each nation's grasp, control over the skies, and their potential military capability, became vital. **Each nation vied to send the first man into space.**

SPUTNIK

The USSR's "fellow traveler" *Sputnik 1* was the first satellite, launched on October 4, 1957.

Its successor, ***Sputnik 2*, was launched on November 3, 1957**, carrying Laika, a dog that became the first living creature in space.

CHAIRMAN MAO AND COMMUNIST CHINA

*One name is synonymous with Communist China—that of Mao Zedong,
a peasant revolutionary turned charismatic leader.*

TIMELINE

- **December 26, 1893** Born in Shaoshan, Hunan Province, China

- **1921** Becomes a founding member of the Chinese Communist Party

- **1927** As nationalists control northern China, Mao retreats to southeast China

- **1934** Leads the Long March

- **1937–45** China unites to fight Japan but later descends into civil war

- **1949** Declares the People's Republic of China

- **1958** The Great Leap Forward

- **1966** The Cultural Revolution

- **1967** Uses martial law to try to reassert power

- **September 9, 1976** Dies in Beijing

THE LONG MARCH

Mao led his followers on a **6,000-mile trek** to establish a new base in northwest China, away from the Kuomintang nationalists.

MAO'S CHINA

All industry was nationalized and farms were organized into collectives. Everyone—men, women, and children—wore the same Zhongshan "Mao" suit.

THE GREAT LEAP FORWARD

Mao's **attempt to mobilize the masses** to greater production actually **had the opposite effect** and, combined with bad harvests, led to economic crisis, famine, and death.

THE GREAT PROLETARIAN CULTURAL REVOLUTION

Blaming "impure" elements of society for the failure of the Great Leap Forward, **Mao sought to purge China of bourgeois values.** Paramilitary Red Guards attacked the elderly and intellectuals, seizing property, torturing, burning, and destroying precious artifacts.

About **1.5 MILLION PEOPLE DIED IN THE CULTURAL REVOLUTION** and much of China's 2,000-year cultural history was destroyed.

THE LITTLE RED BOOK

A personality cult grew around Mao, culminating in the publication of *Quotations from Chairman Mao Zedong.* Ownership of a copy was wise for any citizen wishing to remain alive during the Cultural Revolution.

267
Aphorisms in the Little Red Book written by Mao

1 BILLION
Copies printed

INDIAN INDEPENDENCE

Under the East India Company, India had faced corruption, violence, and heavy taxes.
The British government took direct control in 1857 but the Indian people wanted to rule themselves.

TIMELINE

- **1885** Indian National Congress founded

- **1919** A massacre of Sikhs in Amritsar foments already seething anger

- **1920** Mahatma Gandhi launches an anti-British civil disobedience campaign

- **1939** India is drafted in to fight in World War II

- **1940** The Lahore Resolution is adopted

- **1942** Nehru and Gandhi are arrested for adopting Quit India

- **1946** Lord Mountbatten, the last Viceroy, is sent to transfer power to India

- **August 15, 1947** Indian Independence is granted; hundreds of thousands die during the partition of Pakistan from India

INDIAN NATIONAL CONGRESS

Led by Mahatma Gandhi and Jawaharlal Nehru, the INC was **strongly opposed to the war**.

MUSLIM LEAGUE

Led by Muhammad Ali Jinnah, the League **supported the British**, hoping to get a good settlement after the war. Concerned about a majority Hindu government, they embraced **the Lahore Resolution, a plan to create the separate Islamic state of Pakistan**.

QUIT INDIA

Quit India was a civil disobedience movement based on the spiritual beliefs of *ahimsa* **(nonviolence)** and *satyagraha* **(the quest for truth)**.

NONVIOLENT PROTEST INCLUDED:

- Strikes
- Buying Indian-made clothing
- DIY salt (avoiding taxes)
- Disobeying British laws

Although Gandhi was fiercely against violence, many of his supporters clashed with groups from other religions.

The postwar British government saw imperialism as an expense and wanted rid of India. It felt the easiest way to do it was to partition the country.

PARTITION

The man appointed to divide the country had never set foot on the subcontinent and only flew over the area in a plane once. **Thousands of Sikhs were caught in the middle of land roughly divided into majority Hindus and Muslims.**

17 MILLION
Sikhs, Muslims, and Hindus stranded in the "wrong" country

1 MILLION
People killed in violence in the first year after Independence Day

MAHATMA GANDHI

One of the most recognizable figures from twentieth-century history, the "Father of India" was a nonviolent figurehead in a very violent struggle for Indian independence.

TIMELINE

October 2, 1869 Born in Porbandar, India, as Mohandas Karamchand Gandhi

1888 Sails to England to study law in London

1893–1914 Works as a lawyer in South Africa, where he develops the strategy of peaceful protest

1897 Assaulted by a white mob in Durban, but refuses to press charges

1906 Indians hold mass protest at Johannesburg under Gandhi's leadership

1920 After a massacre of 400 Sikhs, Gandhi remolds the Indian National Congress and begins campaigning for independence from Britain

1922–24 Serves two years of a six-year prison sentence for sedition

---
MAHATMA
= "Great Soul"

EARLY LIFE

Gandhi's father was chief minister of Porbandar in western India. His mother was devoutly religious. **Although Hindu, he was also brought up in the influence of Jainism, a specifically nonviolent religion.**

SOUTH AFRICA

Gandhi led nonviolent resistance to racial discrimination in South Africa. Hundreds of Indians, including Gandhi himself, went to jail, were flogged, and were even shot before temporary peace was negotiated by Gandhi.

APARIGRAHA

Meaning "nonpossession" in Sanskrit, Gandhi's *aparigraha* saw him **reject material goods**, money, and property. *Samabhava* (equability) allowed him to **accept anything, good or bad, that came his way**.

PARTITION

One of Gandhi's greatest sorrows was that an **independent India was also a divided one**. He desperately tried to quell the violence.

1930 Organizes a Salt March against British-imposed taxes

1931 Attends a conference in London and is imprisoned on his return

1932 Goes on hunger strike

1934 Resigns from the Congress Party to fight for the rural poor

1939 Strongly opposes World War II

1942 Gandhi's Quit India policy demands British withdrawal

1945 India is granted independence but partitioned

January 30, 1948 Assassinated by a Hindu fanatic

60,000
People imprisoned after the Salt March

KOREAN WAR

The end of World War II left Korea, formerly occupied by Japan, divided. In a three-year battle between north and south, thousands lost their lives.

 DATES JUNE 25, 1950–JULY 27, 1953

 LOCATION FRONTLINE AT THE 38TH PARALLEL, KOREA

 COMBATANTS NORTH KOREA VS SOUTH KOREA

 CASUALTIES ESTIMATES VARY WILDLY: THE UN ESTIMATES 3 MILLION KOREANS, 900,000 CHINESE, AND 33,629 AMERICANS DIED; OTHER NATIONS' LOSSES WERE IN THE THOUSANDS

 RESULT KOREA IS STILL DIVIDED

TIMELINE

38°

1945
Korea is divided along the 38th parallel division of latitude, 38 degrees north of the equator

1948
The anticommunist Republic of Korea is established in South Korea, supported by the U.S. government

In the North, communist Kim Il Sung declares the Democratic People's Republic of Korea, backed by the Soviet Union

1950
June 25 The North Korean army invades South Korea

June 27 The United Nations Security Council passes Resolution 83, calling on member states to send military aid to South Korea

THE HIDDEN ENEMY

Soldiers had to fight the weather too. Arctic winters, tropical summers, and devastating monsoons claimed many lives.

PRISONERS OF WAR

More than **1,000 UN POWS** suffered horrific conditions, **torture**, and **starvation**.

UN FORCES INCLUDED:

• U.S. • Britain • Australia • • Canada • New Zealand • Netherlands • Turkey • Philippines • France • India

PROPAGANDA

Both sides produced propaganda, but mainly the Chinese, who sent leaflets, banners, cards, and gifts. Porcelain doves of peace were eagerly collected by soldiers as souvenirs.

September 15 The U.S. Army's X Corps lands; Seoul is liberated ten days later

October 25 China enters the war

1951
January 4 Seoul is recaptured by China

March 14 Seoul is again liberated, by the UN

July 10 Truce talks begin but hostilities continue

1953
July 27 A ceasefire agreement is reached but Korea remains divided

THE CONQUEST OF EVEREST

For millennia the highest mountain on Earth was believed unclimbable. In 1953 two men proved the world wrong, but they, too, would have failed without their massive team.

TIMELINE

May 29 29,029 ft.—Hillary and Tenzing spend fifteen minutes on the summit from 11:30 a.m.

May 21 26,000 ft.—The "death zone", where there is not enough oxygen for life

May 20 24,500 ft.

May 17 24,000 ft.

May 4 23,000 ft.

May 3 22,000 ft.

May 1 21,300 ft.

April 22 20,200 ft.

April 15—Climbers reach 19,400 ft.

April 12—Base camp established at 17,900 ft.

March 10, 1953—Expedition sets out

THE TEAM

Led by Colonel John Hunt, the team included **11 British mountaineers, 2 New Zealanders, 20 guides** from the Sherpa community, **362 porters,** a correspondent from the *Times* newspaper **and a herd of yaks**.

It set out from Kathmandu with **10,000 LBS.** of supplies.

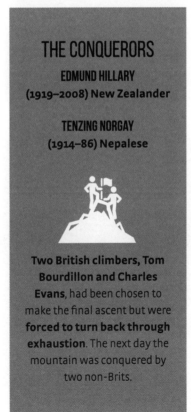

THE CONQUERORS

EDMUND HILLARY
(1919–2008) New Zealander

TENZING NORGAY
(1914–86) Nepalese

Two British climbers, **Tom Bourdillon and Charles Evans**, had been chosen to make the final ascent but were **forced to turn back through exhaustion**. The next day the mountain was conquered by two non-Brits.

News reached Great Britain in time to be released on the **morning of June 2, Queen Elizabeth II's coronation day**. A scoop for the *Times*, it was the last secret-coded message to be relayed by runner.

THE CORONATION OF QUEEN ELIZABETH II

In February 1952 King George VI died, making his daughter, Elizabeth, Queen. Her coronation in 1953 marked a bright, new beginning for a war-ravaged nation.

  DATE JUNE 2, 1953

BEGINS 11:15 A.M.

  GUESTS 8,251

NATIONS REPRESENTED 129

 DURATION NEARLY THREE HOURS

Elizabeth was not born to be Queen, but the abdication of her uncle Edward VIII had made her father King. The royal family was hugely popular for the role they had played in World War II.

TELEVISION

Elizabeth's was to be **the first televised coronation**. Most people did not have a set, but as anticipation reached fever pitch, TVs flew off the shelves and neighbors crowded around a single set.

STREET PARTIES

Continuing a trend set at the end of World War II, many people had street parties. Britain was still heavily rationed, but **households were allowed an extra 1 lb. of sugar and 4 oz. of margarine.** Trestle tables were decorated in red, white, and blue.

THE CEREMONY

The **Archbishop of Canterbury presided at Westminster Abbey**, site of coronations for 900 years. Elizabeth, the 39th sovereign to be crowned (and the sixth queen), wore a **dress of white satin** embroidered with emblems of the United Kingdom and Commonwealth, which was **designed by Norman Hartnell**.

THE CORONATION IN NUMBERS

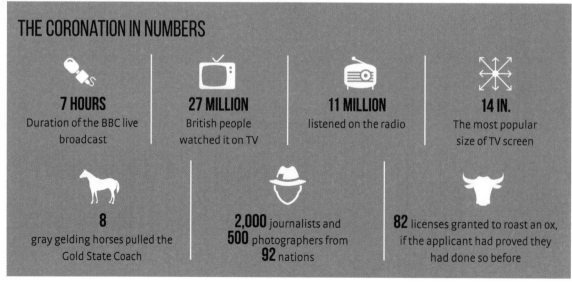

7 HOURS
Duration of the BBC live broadcast

27 MILLION
British people watched it on TV

11 MILLION
listened on the radio

14 IN.
The most popular size of TV screen

8
gray gelding horses pulled the Gold State Coach

2,000 journalists and **500** photographers from **92** nations

82 licenses granted to roast an ox, if the applicant had proved they had done so before

THE HOUSE UN-AMERICAN ACTIVITIES COMMITTEE

As the Cold War intensified, the United States government became increasingly concerned with communist threats from within its own country.

TIMELINE

1938 HUAC is created, charged with identifying, investigating, and trying in a court of law individuals or organizations suspected of having fascist or communist ties

1930s–40s Many HUAC investigations include high-profile entertainers

1950–4 "McCarthyism" reaches its zenith

1960s HUAC's influence wanes

1969 HUAC is renamed the Internal Security Committee

1975 The Committee is dissolved

THE RED MENACE

Americans were **encouraged to believe the threat of communism presented a choice between personal freedom and national security**, though many argued that view went against the First Amendment of the Constitution, which allowed freedom of speech and assembly.

TACTICS

An individual would be subpoenaed and interrogated about their political beliefs. Those refusing to answer could be sent to prison for contempt. They would then be ordered to provide names of others, who would also be grilled.

McCARTHYISM

The practice, begun by **Senator Joseph McCarthy, led to federal government employees being accused of affiliation with communism**. Job losses and blacklisting from future work were frequent. His aggressive tactics were **condemned as unethical by Congress in 1954.**

ALGER HISS

In **1948, government official Alger Hiss was accused of espionage and found guilty**. He served forty-four months in prison but spent the rest of his life trying to prove his innocence.

THE HOLLYWOOD BLACKLIST

10 Names on the original 1947 blacklist

150 Names on the blacklist in 1950

500 People on the graylist of "suspected subversives"

THE HOLLYWOOD TEN

In 1947 **41 screenwriters, directors, and producers were subpoenaed**. Those who answered "yes" to having been a member of the communist party, but could name "fellow travelers", were allowed to continue work.

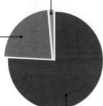

Ten witnesses refused to cooperate. They each received:

- A **$1,000 FINE** ($11,000 or £8,500 today)
- Up to a year in **jail**
- **Banishment** from working in Hollywood

THE FOUR-MINUTE MILE

Until a windy day in 1954, most people believed that running a mile in less than four minutes was beyond human possibility.

 DATE MAY 6, 1954

 LOCATION IFFLEY ROAD TRACK, OXFORD UNIVERSITY, UK

 RUNNER ROGER BANNISTER

 PACEMAKERS CHRIS BRASHER, CHRIS CHATAWAY

 TIME 3 MINUTES 59.4 SECONDS

 SPECTATORS 3,000

ROGER BANNISTER

The **24-year-old medical student** had previously studied at Oxford. Later, in 1954, Bannister retired from running to become a neurologist. **He was knighted in 1975.**

THE RACE

Bannister's **record-breaking attempt was made during the Amateur Athletic Association's annual match at Oxford**. Pacemaker Chris Brasher led the way, then exchanged places with Chris Chataway, who finally allowed Bannister to break out in the last few seconds. Crossing the finish, Bannister collapsed into the arms of a friend.

CAN HUMANS EVER RUN A THREE-MINUTE MILE?

Neither short enough to be a sprint nor long enough to be a paced distance race, mile-running depends on oxygen supply. Runners often run out of oxygen in their lungs and muscles before they run out of energy, making a sub-three-minute mile almost impossible.

WORLD-RECORD BREAKERS SINCE INCLUDE:

3:57.9

JOHN LANDY
Australian
June 1954

3:48.4

STEVE OVETT
British
August 1981

3:47.33

SEBASTIAN COE
British
August 1981

3:46.32

STEVE CRAM
British
July 1985

3:44.39

NOUREDDINE MORCELI
Algerian
September 1993

3:43.13

HICHAM EL GUERROUJ
Moroccan
July 1999

THE FIRST SUCCESSFUL KIDNEY TRANSPLANT

On December 23, 1954, Ronald Herrick donated a kidney to his identical twin brother Richard, who was dying from kidney failure. He had no idea whether the operation would work or if he would even survive himself.

TIMELINE

1954 The world holds its breath as the first kidney transplant is performed at the Peter Bent Brigham Hospital, Boston, by J. E. Murray

1959 Murray performs the first successful transplant between nonidentical twins

1962 Murray successfully transplants a kidney from a cadaver

1990 Murray shares the Nobel Prize with another transplant pioneer, Dr. Edward Donnall Thomas

CONCEPT

Surgeon Joseph Edward Murray (1919–2012) had noticed, while grafting skin onto wounded World War II soldiers, that the **operation only worked on identical twins**. He began to wonder if that might be the key to transplanting internal organs.

PRESS PRESSURE

The media found out just before the operation, quoting doctors who said it was both unethical and doomed to failure.

ETHICAL ISSUES

Murray realized he was asking a healthy person to take a risk solely for the sake of another. He consulted physicians, clergy, and lawyers before suggesting it to the Herrick family. Richard was against the idea.

THE OPERATION

While one team led by Murray prepared Richard, a second team 50 yards away, led by J. Hartwell Harrison, removed one of Ronald's kidneys, then transplanted it into Richard.

23
Age of the twins when they had the operation

17
Tests done to be completely sure the men were identical twins

5.5 HOURS
Length of the procedure

450,000+
Number of kidney transplant operations since performed in the U.S. alone

1 MONTH
Time after the transplant until the twins left hospital

8 YEARS
Extra life Richard Herrick received

56 YEARS
Length of time Ronald survived after the operation, living as a farmer and teacher

ELVIS PRESLEY

Combining the bright music of Bill Haley's Comets with the darker, bluesier roots coming from black musicians, Elvis Presley introduced a new generation of teenagers to rock and roll.

COLD WAR TO PRESENT DAY

TIMELINE

January 8, 1935 Born in Tupelo, Mississippi

1946 Buys his first guitar

1953 Makes a demo of "My Happiness" and "That's When Your Heartaches Begin"

1954 Makes a demo at Sam Phillips's Sun Studio

1955 Managed by Tom Parker, Presley signs a contract with RCA

1956 "Heartbreak Hotel" sells over 1 million copies. Elvis's debut album *Elvis Presley* goes to No.1 in the Billboard chart, he appears on the *Ed Sullivan Show*, and his movie *Love Me Tender* opens

1957 Buys Graceland mansion

1958 Drafted into the U.S. Army

1960 Leaves active service and continues a stellar recording and film career

1968 After a career dip, *The Comeback Special* TV show shoots him straight back to stardom

1969 Live performances in Las Vegas set record attendances

August 16, 1977 Dies in Memphis, Tennessee

EARLY LIFE

Presley's early life was literally dirt-poor— the floor of his family home was bare earth.

ROOTS MUSIC

Presley loved the gospel music he heard in his family's Pentecostal church and the country blues he heard in the Beale Street clubs in Memphis. **Many of his early hits had already been recorded by black artists, who had not received the airplay that, being white, Elvis could enjoy.**

OUTRAGE

TV audiences were shocked at Elvis's hip gyrations. He was often filmed from the waist up.

"COLONEL" TOM PARKER

A former carnival showman, Parker (the "colonel" moniker was a nickname) **managed Presley's career with an iron fist**, taking up to **50 percent** of his client's earnings.

$7.90 The price of Elvis's first guitar

40 The 1973 concert *Elvis: Aloha from Hawaii via Satellite* is beamed to **40 countries** and seen by between **1 and 1.5 billion people**

PELÉ

More formally known as Edson Arantes do Nascimento, Pérola Negra (Black Pearl) may be the most famous athlete in the world.

TIMELINE

- **October 23, 1940** Born in Três Corações, Brazil

- **1956** Initially rejected by major clubs in São Paulo, he finally joins Santos FC

- **1958** Part of the World Cup–winning Brazilian soccer team

- **1962** Part of the World Cup–winning Brazilian soccer team

- **November 20, 1969** In his 909th first-class match, Pelé scores his 1,000th goal

- **1970** Part of the World Cup–winning Brazilian soccer team

- **1974** Announces retirement but agrees to a $7 million contract ($32.7 million or £25 million today) to play with the New York Cosmos

- **1977** The Cosmos win the league championship and Pelé finally retires

- **1978** Wins the International Peace Award for his work with UNICEF

- **1980** Named Athlete of the Century by *L'Equipe* newspaper

- **1999** Named Athlete of the Century by the International Olympic Committee

WON BY SANTOS FOOTBALL CLUB WITH PELÉ AS INSIDE LEFT FORWARD

9 São Paulo league championships

2 major cups

17

Pelé's age when he played his first World Cup

1958 WORLD CUP (SWEDEN)

Pelé scores a hat-trick in the semifinal against France, and two goals in the final where **Brazil beat Sweden 5–2**

1962 WORLD CUP (CHILE)

Pelé tears a leg muscle in his second match but inspires his team to win the tournament

1970 WORLD CUP (MEXICO)

After briefly considering retirement, Pelé scores one of Brazil's goals in their **4–1 win over Italy**

48 HOURS

Length of ceasefire called in the Nigerian Civil War in 1967, so the nation could watch Pelé's visiting team play

THE FIRST MAN IN SPACE

The Cold War brought many bad things to the world, but it also initiated some positives for the human race. Whatever his nationality, the first man in space would become an achievement for all.

 FIRST MAN IN SPACE YURI GAGARIN

 BORN MARCH 9, 1934, IN GZHATSK, SOVIET UNION

 DIED MARCH 27, 1968, NEAR MOSCOW, SOVIET UNION

 PROFESSION TEST PILOT AND INDUSTRIAL TECHNICIAN

 CRAFT *VOSTOK 1*

 DATE APRIL 12, 1961

 MISSION ORBIT THE PLANET

 LAUNCHED BAIKONUR COSMODROME, SOUTHERN KAZAKHSTAN

 ALTITUDE 187 MILES

 TIME 108 MINUTES

SERGEI PAVLOVICH KOROLEV

At the time of becoming chief designer, **Korolev was a prisoner in a labor camp, a victim of one of Joseph Stalin's purges**. Korolev went on to build a rocket that could carry warheads, launch a satellite, *Sputnik 1*, and, among the many other firsts, send the first animal, man, and woman into space.

REACTION

Gagarin became an international celebrity and **hero of the Soviet Union**.

U.S. REACTION

The U.S. was further humiliated in **August 1961** when *Vostok 2*, piloted by cosmonaut **Gherman Titov**, made **seventeen orbits over twenty-five hours in space**.

President John F. Kennedy realized that, in the battle of propaganda, he needed to go one better. On **May 25, 1961**, he announced a new goal: **to put a man on the Moon**.

THE CUBAN MISSILE CRISIS

For a few tense weeks in 1962, the world held its breath as the United States of America and the Soviet Union played a dangerous game of nuclear chicken.

 DATES OCTOBER 14–28, 1962

 LOCATION CUBA

 AGGRESSORS PRESIDENT JOHN F. KENNEDY FOR THE UNITED STATES VS NIKITA KHRUSHCHEV FOR THE SOVIET UNION

 RESULT BOTH SIDES STEP DOWN

TIMELINE

October 14 U.S. spy planes photograph Soviet medium-range missiles in Cuba

October 16 The U.S. National Security Council's Executive Committee (ExComm) meets to discuss possible moves

October 17 Analysis shows Cuba also has long-range missiles

October 18 Soviet foreign minister Andrei Gromyko says missiles are for defense only

October 20 ExComm recommends "quarantining" Cuba

October 22 President Kennedy addresses the nation on television; he tells the Soviets to remove the missiles

BACKGROUND

In April 1961 the CIA launched an **invasion of Cuba at the Bay of Pigs**, carried out by 1,400 Cuban exiles. It was easily **defeated by Castro's revolutionary army**, further damaging relations with President Kennedy's White House.

EXCOMM

The Executive Committee of the National Security Council was **a group of American officials trying to decide the best policy during the crisis**.

AMERICA PREPARES FOR WAR

4 tactical air squadrons readied for air strikes

100,000 troops sent to Florida for possible invasion

180 naval vessels dispatched to the Caribbean

40,000 Marines prepared for action

B-52S loaded with nuclear weapons flew at all times

October 26 ExComm discusses invading Cuba, knowing this could incite war

October 27 U.S. pilot Major Rudolf Anderson is shot down in Soviet airspace, but not on Khrushchev's command; both sides see the danger of the situation

October 27 Kennedy agrees not to invade Cuba if Khrushchev removes Soviet missiles

October 28 On Radio Moscow, Khrushchev agrees to the terms and nuclear war is narrowly avoided

Badly frightened by what might have been, **both sides signed the Partial Nuclear Test Ban Treaty** within a year, and instaled a **hotline between Washington and Moscow**.

THE CONTRACEPTIVE PILL

It's rare that a single medical advance influences an entire generation, but the liberation brought by the contraceptive pill gave millions of women across the world their first genuine choice in life.

 THE "PILL" A HORMONE-BASED, REVERSIBLE CONTRACEPTIVE TAKEN ORALLY

 ALTERNATIVES AT THE TIME CONDOM, DIAPHRAGM, ABSTENTION

 MODUS OPERANDI MIMICS PREGNANCY, FOOLING THE BODY INTO OFFSETTING CONCEPTION

 1916 MARGARET SANGER SENTENCED TO THIRTY DAYS IN JAIL FOR OPENING A BIRTH CONTROL CLINIC

COLD WAR TO PRESENT DAY

TIMELINE

1950s The contraceptive pill is developed by a team led by Dr. Gregory Pincus, funded by Margaret Sanger

1960 Enovid, manufactured by Searle, is approved for use by the U.S.'s Food and Drug Administration

December 4, 1961 The National Health Service approves use in Britain, for married women only

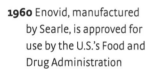 **1.2 MILLION** American women were taking the pill within **two years of its coming onto the market**

 **100 MILLION** women take the pill worldwide

FEMINISM

Freed from a life where having children was not a choice, **women were able to take new roles in the workplace** and, by extension, to **have more say in the way the world is run.**

MORALITY

The pill led to questions of morality, since, in theory, **sex could be indulged in without consequences. Many were against unmarried women having access for this reason.**

FREE LOVE

Some women felt **pressurized into having sex by a "free love"** culture enabled by the pill.

HEALTH SCARES

The pill has been dogged by health scares, especially for women who smoke, but does have some health benefits.

THE PROFUMO AFFAIR

The "Swinging Sixties" saw a James Bond–worthy, sex-and-spies scandal rock the British establishment. The truth about an affair in 1961 that brought down a Cabinet minister has never been satisfactorily revealed.

 ## DRAMATIS PERSONAE

JOHN "JACK" PROFUMO
Secretary of State for War

CHRISTINE KEELER
A showgirl from Murray's Cabaret Club

MANDY RICE-DAVIES
Witness, a friend of Keeler's

STEPHEN WARD
Celebrity osteopath, a mover and shaker nicknamed "The Fixer"

YEVGENY IVANOV
A Soviet naval attaché

SWINGING LONDON

Bouffant-hair, sunglasses, sports cars, and swimming pools—the fast lifestyle enjoyed by Stephen Ward and his latest protégé, Christine Keeler, epitomized the most glamorous city on earth.

GETTING CHILLY

Even as London partied, the Cold War was sending an icy blast through international politics. **Paranoia simmered under the hedonism; anyone could be a spy.**

POOL PARTY

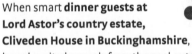

When smart **dinner guests at Lord Astor's country estate, Cliveden House in Buckinghamshire**, heard excited squeals from the pool outside, they rushed outside to find Ward and Keeler.

DANGEROUS LIAISONS

One of the guests, cabinet minister John Profumo, was smitten with Keeler and the two enjoyed a short affair. Unfortunately, Keeler had also been seeing Soviet officer Yevgeny Ivanov.

SCANDAL SHEETS

Profumo's former relationship with Keeler eventually became public, sensationalized by a leering press using national security as an excuse. **Profumo resigned on June 4, 1963.**

Ward, abandoned by his society friends, was tried for procuration. While on bail, he **died from an overdose of sleeping pills**—whether or not by his own hand remains unclear.

6
Number of mourners at Stephen Ward's funeral

2046

Year records relating to the Profumo Affair will be made public

THE CUBAN REVOLUTION

By the 1950s Cuba had been suffering from various unstable governments for half a century, and yet another dictator made the country ripe for revolution.

COLD WAR TO PRESENT DAY

FULGENCIO BATISTA

FIDEL CASTRO

Batista had **conducted a military coup in 1933**, serving as elected President. **In 1952 he led another coup and ruled as dictator.**

Fidel Castro, **a lawyer**, had intended to stand in the 1952 elections. After Batista took power, **Castro vowed to fight against the dictatorship**.

1953
On July 26 a **160-strong attack on an army barracks** led by Fidel Castro and his brother Raúl fails; **the Castro brothers are imprisoned**

1955
Exiled in Mexico, the brothers **meet Ernesto "Che" Guevara**, an Argentinian doctor with revolutionary ideals

1956
Fidel and Raúl Castro and Che Guevara lead seventy-nine armed rebels into Cuba; they are badly defeated and forced to retreat

1957
Student-led protesters attack the Presidential Palace; trades unions call a general strike; bombings and arson attacks whittle at Batista's government

1958
America embargoes weapon exports to Cuba, weakening Batista's rule

In **Operation Verano**, **Batista** attacks Castro's growing forces but is **defeated at the Battle of La Plata**

Che Guevara's rebels capture the city of Santa Clara

1959
January 1 Batista flees Cuba
January 3 Guevara leads the revolutionary army into Havana, unopposed
February 16 Fidel Castro is sworn in as Prime Minister

> ### THE 26TH OF JULY MOVEMENT
> Named for the failed 1953 army-barracks attack, the Castro brothers' guerrilla campaign began from a base in the Sierra Mountains

CUBA UNDER BATISTA

600,000 Cubans unemployed
46% land owned by **1.5%** of the population

In Cuba, American corporations owned:

80% utilities
90% mines
40% sugar plantations
50% railroads

CUBA UNDER CASTRO

- **600** people from the Batista government executed by the revolutionary courts
- Any land parcel larger than **1,000** acres was taken by the state
- American-owned companies were **nationalized**

Fidel Castro would rule Cuba from 1959 to 2008. At first he was welcomed by the United States, but, after Cuba began to work with the Soviet Union, relations quickly soured.

ASSASSINATION OF JFK

On November 22, 1963, President John F. Kennedy was in a motorcade traveling through the center of Dallas, Texas. At 12:30 p.m., the motorcade was in Dealey Plaza, just outside the downtown area, when several gunshots were fired.

WHO WAS INJURED?

JFK was wounded in the back and the throat, and, fatally, in the head.

Governor John Connally, who was sitting directly in front of Kennedy, sustained three wounds to his rib, wrist and thigh.

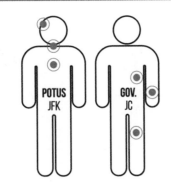

WHO WAS RESPONSIBLE?

- The shots came from the **sixth floor** of the Texas School Book Depository. A "sniper's nest" and rifle were found there, along with **three spent cartridge shells**.
- **Lee Harvey Oswald** was working as a temporary employee at the Book Depository.
- Oswald was **arrested in a movie theater**, less than **ninety minutes after** JFK's shooting, and was charged with killing Kennedy and a **police officer named John Tippit**.
- Oswald was himself **shot by nightclub operator Jack Ruby** while being transferred from the city jail to Dallas county jail.
- A 1979 U.S. House Committee inquiry found Kennedy was **"probably assassinated as a result of a conspiracy"** and that there was a "high probability" a second gunman as well as Oswald fired at the President.

THE AFTERMATH

- On November 24, JFK's funeral cortege moved from the White House to the Capitol. This was **modeled on the funeral of Abraham Lincoln**, at Mrs. Kennedy's request.
- **250,000** people came to pay their respects
- On November 25, JFK was laid to rest at Arlington National Cemetery. The funeral was **attended by representatives from more than 100 countries**.
- On November 29, 1963, President Johnson appointed the President's Commission on the Assassination of President Kennedy, a.k.a. **the Warren Commission**.

THE END OF JFK

12:30 P.M.
JFK and Governor Connally are shot

12:34 P.M.
The first news wire service announcement of the shooting is broadcast

12:38 P.M.
Mrs. Kennedy holds her husband's body as his blood runs onto her clothes; "They've murdered my husband," she says

1:00 P.M.
Doctors at Parkland Memorial Hospital declare JFK dead

1:26 P.M.
JFK's body is returned to *Air Force One*

1:30 P.M.
The official announcement of his death is made

2:38 P.M.
Vice-president Lyndon B. Johnson is sworn in as President; he insists the bloodstained Jackie stand beside him during the ceremony

BEATLEMANIA

In 1963 four young men from Liverpool began to attract fan worship eclipsing even that enjoyed by bobby-soxer Frank Sinatra and the king of rock 'n' roll Elvis Presley.

THE FAB FOUR

JOHN LENNON
GUITAR, VOCALS, MAIN SONGWRITER

PAUL McCARTNEY
BASS GUITAR, VOCALS, MAIN SONGWRITER

GEORGE HARRISON
GUITAR, VOCALS, SONGWRITER

RINGO STARR
DRUMS, VOCALS, SONGWRITER

BEATLEMANIA TIMELINE

1962

October "Love Me Do," the Beatles' first single, reaches No.17

1963

January First No.1 single: "Please Please Me"
November First million-selling album: *With the Beatles*

1964

February Beatlemania crosses the Atlantic as the group tour and appear on the Ed Sullivan TV show
July The band's first movie, *A Hard Day's Night*, is released
December Their fourth album immediately goes to No.1

1966

August The group's final official concert takes place in San Francisco

The Beatles formed in Liverpool in 1960 and their early music appealed to teenage fans, who followed them with almost obsessional intensity.

FANDEMONIUM

The phrase **"Beatlemania"** was first coined by *Mirror* journalist Don Short in 1963, after he witnessed frenzied screaming as the band played on the British TV program *Sunday Night at the London Palladium.*

EXPERIMENTATION

- Partly to avoid the screaming, **the Beatles became a studio band, and as their music matured,** some of the more hysterical devotion mellowed.
- Some fans grew with their idols, but albums like *Rubber Soul, Revolver* and *Sgt. Pepper's Lonely Hearts Club Band* also brought new aficionados.
- The band's final performance, in **January 1969**, was about as far from fans as it could be—**on the roof of their London company, Apple Corps**.
- A discreet announcement on **April 10, 1970**, told the world **the Beatles were no more**.

WHEN HERO WORSHIP TURNS BAD

Most of the Beatles' fans were harmless, but on **December 8, 1980**, the world was shocked when **Mark David Chapman shot John Lennon**, with whom he had become obsessed.

THE VIETNAM WAR

The Vietnam War between communist north Vietnam—supported by the People's Republic of China and the Soviet Union—and south Vietnam—supported by anticommunist countries, mainly the U.S.—felt like a proxy Cold War.

DATES NOVEMBER 1, 1955–APRIL 30, 1975

LOCATION THE JUNGLES OF VIETNAM

CASUALTIES MORE THAN 58,000 AMERICAN GIs AND MILLIONS OF VIETNAMESE, BOTH COMBATANTS AND CIVILIANS

RESULT SOUTH VIETNAM SURRENDERED AND THE COUNTRY WAS UNIFIED AS THE SOCIALIST REPUBLIC OF VIETNAM; AMERICA WITHDREW IN 1973, HAVING LOST PRESTIGE AND THOUSANDS OF YOUNG MEN

BUILD-UP

Communist Ho Chi Minh wanted the Vietnamese people to govern themselves, but the Allies said Vietnam should return to French control. **The country split into north and south.**

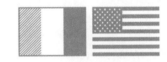

FRENCH RETREAT

Ho Chi Minh declared war to unite the country. Fearing another communist nation, America took a direct role. The first **U.S. combat troops arrived in 1965**.

19

Average age of American soldiers

DIFFERENT RULES

The war was extremely difficult to fight using traditional Western tactics. In the dense jungle and rice paddies, GIs could not even find their enemy—**the southern rebels called Viet Cong**—and **U.S. forces floundered in the face of guerrilla tactics**.

UNPOPULAR WAR

Back home, people saw the human cost of the war and public opinion turned against the conflict.

7 MILLION

Bombs dropped on Vietnam, Laos, and Cambodia

TERRIFYING WEAPONS

U.S.: Napalm, toxic chemicals such as Agent Orange, the M14 rifle

Viet Cong: Tunnels, booby traps, AK-47 rifle

THE CIVIL RIGHTS MOVEMENT

By the 1950s and 1960s, black Americans were extremely angry about the discrimination they faced in daily life. Slavery might have been abolished, but segregation was still enshrined in law.

COLD WAR TO PRESENT DAY

TIMELINE

- **1955** Rosa Parks refuses to give up her bus seat

- **1956** Boycott of the Montgomery bus system

- **1957** The Little Rock Nine; black students at a formerly segregated school need federal troops to escort them to class

- **1957** The Civil Rights Act allows prosecution of anyone trying to prevent people voting

- **1960** The Greensboro sit-in; four African American students refuse to leave a segregated Woolworths lunch counter until they are served, sparking a sit-in movement

- **1963** The March on Washington takes place, during which Martin Luther King Jr. delivers his "I Have a Dream" speech

1967 DETROIT RIOT

- **43** deaths
- **1,000** burned buildings
- **7,000** arrests

JIM CROW LAWS

In the South, black Americans had separate, usually inferior public facilities, towns, and schools to white people. **Interracial marriage was banned** and literary laws ensured **many black people couldn't vote**. Life was better in the northern states but black people still faced discrimination.

ROSA PARKS

(1913–2005)

Returning home from work on **December 1, 1955**, Parks **refused to give up her place**, in the "black seats" at the back of the bus, to a white passenger. **She was arrested**, sparking outrage.

MALCOLM X

(1925–65)

While in prison for petty crime, **Malcolm Little joined the Nation of Islam** and became an inspiring leader, articulating the anger felt by African Americans. **Advocating civil rights by "any means necessary,"** he inspired the Black Power movement.

- **1964** The Civil Rights Act guarantees equal employment and integrated public facilities

- **1965** On Bloody Sunday in Selma, Alabama, 600 peaceful demonstrators are attacked by police; dozens are hospitalized

- **1965** The Voting Rights Act bans voter literacy tests

- **1965** Malcolm X is assassinated

- **1965** The Watts riots in Los Angeles see clashes between protesters and police, resulting in thirty-four deaths, 1,000 injured and $40 million of damage

- **1966** The Black Panther Party is founded

- **1968** Martin Luther King Jr. is assassinated

In 2008 **Barack Obama** was elected **the first black President of the United States**. The fight for civil rights, however, continues.

DR. MARTIN LUTHER KING JR.

Given by possibly the best known civil rights activist of all time, Martin Luther King's speeches are still widely quoted today.

TIMELINE

January 15, 1929 Born in Atlanta, Georgia

1944 Enters Morehouse College in Atlanta; on vacation in the north, he realizes not all of the U.S. is segregated

1955 Earns a doctorate from Boston University

1956 Leads the Montgomery Bus Boycott

1959 Traveling to India, King is impressed by Gandhi's peaceful campaign methods

1963 Helps organize the March on Washington; he is arrested

1964 Becomes the youngest person to receive the Nobel Peace Prize

1964 The Civil Rights Act is passed

1968 Assassinated on April 4 in Memphis, Tennessee

THE MONTGOMERY BUS BOYCOTT

Following Rosa Parks's refusal to yield her seat to a white passenger, **King led a boycott of buses until segregation ended**. His stirring oration helped win the cause.

KING'S SPEECHES

The most **powerful weapon** King deployed **was his voice**. Although letters, such as the one he sent from Birmingham jail, were eloquent, his speeches inspired all who heard them. **"I Have a Dream"** and **"I've Been to the Mountaintop"** are still taught in schools.

AIMS OF THE MARCH ON WASHINGTON INCLUDED:

- An end to segregation in schools
- An end to police abuse of black people
- An end of discrimination in the workplace

250,000
people attended the **March on Washington**

OPPOSITION

Some civil rights activists, such as Malcolm X, believed King's tactics were too passive and called for more militant action.

ASSASSINATION

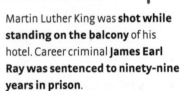

Martin Luther King was **shot while standing on the balcony** of his hotel. Career criminal **James Earl Ray was sentenced to ninety-nine years in prison**.

Every third Monday of January is Martin Luther King Jr. Day, a federal vacation in the U.S.

730 streets in the U.S. are named after Martin Luther King Jr.

THE RISE OF THE MINISKIRT

Nothing sums up the youthful optimism of the "Swinging Sixties" like the miniskirt.

COLD WAR TO PRESENT DAY

TIMELINE

1920s Skirts are the shortest for millennia; hemlines fall again in the 1930s

1926 Economist George Taylor coins the term "hemline index," equating the length of skirts to prices on the stock exchange

1957 Mary Quant opens her store "Bazaar" in Chelsea's King's Road

1962 Quant signs a contract with American department store J. C. Penney; she begins experimenting with hemlines and bright colors

1965 André Courrèges includes a short skirt in his spring/summer collection; John Bates designs short-skirted costumes for Diana Rigg in TV series *The Avengers*

1966 Mary Quant introduces miniskirts, named for her favorite car, the Mini Cooper

1968 Jackie Kennedy wears a short skirt when marrying Aristotle Onassis

RENAISSANCE

The 1960s was ready for the miniskirt. **Young people wanted to be free of their parents' stuffy, colorless world**. Music was changing, the world was changing, and the arrival of the birth control pill meant **attitudes were changing**.

The title of "inventor" of the miniskirt is contested. Most agree Parisian couturier **André Courrèges** and British designer **Mary Quant** worked on the concept independently and simultaneously.

STYLE CHOICES

Courrèges's skirt was angular and stiff, designed to be worn with bare legs, while **Quant took advantage of the newly invented pantyhose**. Flat shoes or knee-length boots sent a saucy, mixed message of flirtation and innocence.

NEW MATERIALS

- Quant loved manmade fibers and **was the first to use PVC in clothing**.
- Not everyone loved the mini. **Coco Chanel thought it awful** and some countries, especially in Africa, banned it.

C.7 MILLION

Number of sixties women who had at **least one Mary Quant product** in their wardrobes

6–7

Number of **inches above the knee** on Mary Quant's skirts

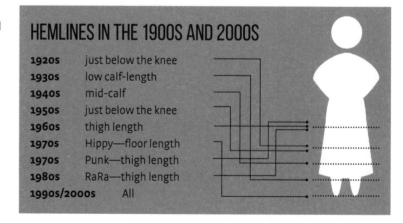

HEMLINES IN THE 1900S AND 2000S

1920s	just below the knee
1930s	low calf-length
1940s	mid-calf
1950s	just below the knee
1960s	thigh length
1970s	Hippy—floor length
1970s	Punk—thigh length
1980s	RaRa—thigh length
1990s/2000s	All

KATHRINE SWITZER'S BOSTON MARATHON

The Boston Marathon is one of the most popular amateur running events in the world. In 1967 it was open to all runners—if they were men.

 DATE APRIL 19, 1967

 LOCATION BOSTON

 REGISTERED K. V. SWITZER

 RUNNER KATHRINE SWITZER (BORN 1947), AMERICAN JOURNALIST AND AMATEUR RUNNER

Switzer's coach believed women were too fragile to run marathons. Undeterred, she registered to run the Boston Marathon. **The Amateur Athletic Union's rule book didn't mention gender,** so she didn't know she was breaking any rules.

At about mile four, **a race official began shouting at her and trying to rip the race number from her vest**. She got away, even though he was dragging at her shirt, and the press cameras clicked.

Shocked and terrified, **she completed the race**, despite being heckled by the press, abused by the official, and having an argument with her boyfriend.

The images of Switzer being accosted are **some of the most famous photographs in sports history**. They have angered and inspired millions of women since.

AFTER THE RACE

Switzer campaigned for official statutes for women in distance races and continues to inspire sportswomen today. **The Boston Marathon finally accepted female entrants in 1972.**

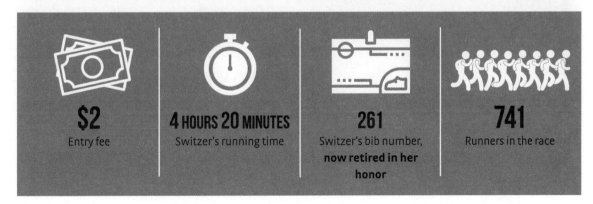

$2
Entry fee

4 HOURS 20 MINUTES
Switzer's running time

261
Switzer's bib number, **now retired in her honor**

741
Runners in the race

THE SUMMER OF LOVE

There was something in the air in the summer of 1967—and not all of it may have been entirely legal. Times had been a-changing for a while but, as psychedelia merged with hippie love, and youth turned on, tuned in, and dropped out, suddenly the world noticed.

HAPPENINGS

Events—some planned, some not—**took place mainly in London and San Francisco**, as a communal burst of creativity surged through the heat. Some experimented with hallucinogenic drugs such as LSD.

ALL YOU NEED

Public gatherings **focusing on meditation, love, music, and sex became known as love-ins**. The first was held in **March or April 1967, in Elysian Park, Los Angeles**.

DRUG CULTURE

In June **Mick Jagger and Keith Richards of the Rolling Stones went to prison for drug offenses**. Their sentences were overturned after public protest.

PROTEST AND SURVIVE

100,000

Estimated number of **anti-Vietnam War protestors at the Washington Monument in October**. Others publicly burned their draft cards.

SGT. PEPPER'S LONELY HEARTS CLUB BAND

Released by the Beatles on June 1, the album's unique selling point was the band using their recording studio as a creative tool.

£3,000

Cost of the cover art by Peter Blake and Jann Haworth **(£53,500 or $69,000 today)**.

£100

Cost of a regular album cover **(£1,800 or $2,300 today)**.

ON THE BILL

The Monterey International Pop Festival—widely regarded as the beginning of the **Summer of Love**—took place in California on **June 16–18**, with a line-up including:

JIMI HENDRIX

THE WHO

SCOTT MCKENZIE

RAVI SHANKAR

JANIS JOPLIN

OTIS REDDING

THE MAMAS & THE PAPAS

SIMON & GARFUNKEL

THE BYRDS

JEFFERSON AIRPLANE

GRATEFUL DEAD

THE MOON LANDINGS

In 1969 the Space Race reached its dazzling zenith as thousands of dollars, three lives, and American national pride were all staked on one giant leap.

APOLLO 11 MISSION TIMELINE

- **July 16, 09:32 Eastern Daylight Time (EDT)**
  Apollo 11 is launched at Cape Kennedy

- **July 19, 17:21 Universal Time Coordinated (UTC)**
  The astronauts orbit the Moon several times

- **July 20, 17:44 UTC** *Eagle*, the lunar module containing Aldrin and Armstrong, is separated from *Columbia*, the command module; descent begins

- **20:17 UTC** *Eagle* lands at the Sea of Tranquility on the surface of the Moon

- **July 21, 21:34 UTC** *Eagle* leaves the Moon, and successfully docks with *Columbia*

- **July 22, 00:01 UTC** *Eagle* is jettisoned and *Columbia* heads home

- **July 24, 12:50 EDT** The command module enters Earth's atmosphere, thirty-six minutes late

- **16:44 EDT** The crew splashes down safely into the Pacific Ocean

THE CREW

NEIL ARMSTRONG
Mission Commander, first man on the Moon

EDWIN "BUZZ" ALDRIN
Lunar Module Pilot

MICHAEL COLLINS
Command Module Pilot

STEVE BALES
Guidance Officer at Mission Control in Houston

COMPUTER OVERLOAD

During the descent to the Moon's surface, a number of alarms sounded as the computer overloaded, and Armstrong was forced to take semimanual control.

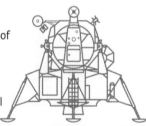

21
Number of **days** the **crew remained in quarantine** to ensure they hadn't brought disease back with them

MAN ALONE

Michael Collins orbited the Moon in the command module for **twenty-one hours**. His greatest fear was something happening to Armstrong and Aldrin, and his having to return alone.

THE STONEWALL RIOTS

A surprise police raid on a popular gay bar in Greenwich Village proved to be the tipping point for grievances that had been bubbling under the surface for many years.

  DATE JUNE 28, 1969

LOCATION STONEWALL INN, NEW YORK CITY

 COMBATANTS PATRONS OF THE BAR AND LOCAL RESIDENTS VS NEW YORK CITY POLICE

 RESULT THE STONEWALL RIOTS SERVE AS A CATALYST FOR THE GAY RIGHTS MOVEMENT

Homosexuality or any form of "sexual deviance" was not tolerated in the 1960s or the decades before. Solicitation of homosexual relations was illegal in New York City in 1969.

THE STONEWALL INN

Run as **a private "bottle bar,"** the **Stonewall Inn** provided sanctuary to LGBT people and welcomed cross-dressers.

THE RAID

Armed with a warrant, **the police raided the Inn, ostensibly for selling liquor without a license.** Employees and patrons were handled roughly. It was the third such incident in a short time.

THE RIOT BEGINS

After the raid, angry patrons and local residents did not disperse. When a lesbian patron was hit over the head, other patrons began **throwing missiles at the police, who barricaded themselves inside the bar**.

FIRE

The crowd set fire to the Inn. It was put out by the fire department, and the riot squad dispersed the angry protesters, but **the riots would continue for five more days**.

MISSILES INCLUDED:

- Pennies
- Cobblestones
- Bottles

Stonewall didn't begin radical activism, but it **became a symbol** of united resistance to the discrimination and persecution LGBT people had suffered for decades.

3

In NYC people could be **arrested** for not wearing at least **three gender-appropriate** articles of clothing

13

People arrested in the raid

400

Approximate number of rioters

2016

President Obama designated the Inn and surrounding streets a **national monument**

APOLLO 13

Unlucky for some, the Apollo program's thirteenth voyage to the Moon could have ended in tragedy. Instead, hard work, innovation, and bravery turned it into NASA's finest hour.

TIMELINE

APRIL 11, 1970
(Hours into the mission)

00:00 *Apollo 13* launched at 13:13, defying superstition

APRIL 14
55:53 A routine procedure causes a decrease in pressure in oxygen tank 1, followed by an electrical short in tank 2 and a fuel-cell failure

56:33 Emergency power-down

58:40 The lunar module *Aquarius* is powered up for the first time; the crew live here until they can return to Earth; nonessential equipment is turned off

APRIL 17
140:10 Command module *Odyssey's* power-up is begun, in an order devised to use minimal power

142:40 *Apollo 13* begins reentry

142:50 Voice contact is established

MAJOR FIGURES

JIM LOVELL
Mission Commander

FRED HAISE
Lunar Module Pilot

JACK SWIGERT
Command Module Pilot

GENE KRANZ
Flight Director, Mission Control

Apollo 13's **first fifty-five hours ran smoothly**, but a routine oxygen-tank stir set off **a chain of disastrous events**. Abandoning hopes of reaching the Moon, **the mission became one of rescue**, with controllers, technicians, engineers, and fellow astronauts working together to find solutions no one had ever considered.

KIT

New equipment was fashioned using only materials that could be found on board.

FILM ADAPTATION

The movie *Apollo 13*, starring Tom Hanks, is widely praised for its accuracy.

THE ARAB OIL EMBARGO

In 1973 oil-producing Arab countries imposed a temporary ban on shipments to the United States, Netherlands, Portugal, and South Africa. The disruption caused ripples worldwide.

COLD WAR TO PRESENT DAY

TIMELINE

1973

October 6 Egypt and Syria launch an attack on Israel on the Jewish holy day of Yom Kippur; Israel retaliated, pushing into Egyptian and Syrian territory, supported by the U.S. and other countries

October 19 OAPEC imposes an oil embargo on the U.S., hoping to force Israel to retreat

1974

March Negotiations lead to the lifting of the ban but the high prices remain

Price of oil in October 1973, before the embargo

$2.90 per barrel

Price in January 1974

$11.65 per barrel

OTHER CONTRIBUTING FACTORS

Although **the Yom Kippur War was the inciting incident**, the oil-producing countries were already angry that the **U.S.'s President Nixon had released the dollar from the gold standard**. This devalued the currency and, since oil was priced in dollars, **reduced what producers received**. The ban was effective because the **developed world had become heavily reliant on cheap oil**.

OAPEC

The **Organization of Petroleum Exporting Countries (OPEC) was formed in 1960** to support member countries' interests and coordinate oil prices and production. **OAPEC (Organization of Arab Petroleum Exporting Countries) was formed in 1968.**

OPEC claims about **four-fifths** of the world's petroleum reserves and **two-fifths** of world oil production.

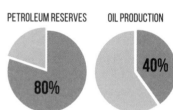

PETROLEUM RESERVES — 80%

OIL PRODUCTION — 40%

U.S. RESPONSE

The U.S. government was forced to ration fuel and impose speed limits to reduce consumption. Nixon considered military action as a last resort, but negotiations were successful.

AFTERMATH

Prices continued to soar and, realizing how reliant they had become on Middle Eastern oil, countries began increasing domestic production and working toward greater energy efficiency.

55 MPH
Speed limit imposed on U.S. highways

10
Gallons of gas allowed per customer during rationing

THE WATERGATE SCANDAL

Caught trying to cover up his own role in a seedy conspiracy, President Richard Nixon abused his presidential power. It led to his downfall and the American people's disillusionment.

TIMELINE

1972

June 17 Five burglars are arrested in the office of the Democratic National Committee

October 10 The *Washington Post* connects Nixon with the burglary conspiracy

November 7 Voters believe Nixon's sworn statement that he is innocent; he wins the election

1973

July 23 Nixon refuses to cede recordings to Special Investigator Archibald Cox's investigation

October 20 The Saturday Night Massacre sees three officials refuse to fire Archibald Cox, then resign

1974

March 1 A grand jury declares Nixon an "unindicted coconspirator"

April 30 The White House releases redacted tapes

July 24 The Supreme Court orders Nixon to hand over the tapes

July 27 The House of Representatives votes to impeach Nixon

July 31 The surrendered tapes conclusively prove Nixon's guilt

August 8 Nixon resigns

BACKGROUND

America was deeply divided over the Vietnam War and tactics used in the 1972 election campaign were brutal.

The **Committee to Re-Elect the President**, known as **CREEP, had bugged the Democratic campaign HQ** and stolen documents. When the tap failed to work, they returned and were caught red-handed.

COVER-UP

Nixon paid hush money to the burglars and instructed the CIA to block the FBI investigation, obstructing justice.

THE CRIME UNRAVELS

Suspecting foul play, *Washington Post* reporters **Bob Woodward and Carl Bernstein started to investigate**.

WHISTLEBLOWER

An anonymous whistleblower, later revealed to be FBI agent **Mark Felt**, sent information to the journalists.

NIXON'S ACHILLES HEEL

Nixon had secretly taped his conversations with the conspirators. He tried to use his executive privilege as President to prevent them being played.

THE SATURDAY NIGHT MASSACRE

Nixon asked three separate officials to fire special prosecutor Archibald Cox on the night of October 20, after Cox continued to demand access to information. All refused and resigned instead.

PUNK ROCK

*There had been many angry bands, making much angry music, but
nothing approached the nihilism of punk rock.*

TIMELINE

● **1960s** Bands such as the
Stooges and Velvet
Underground break the
traditional music mold

● **1973** Legendary nightclub
CBGB opens in
Manhattan's East
Village, creating not
just a sound, but a
look—and an attitude

● **1974** Malcolm McLaren and
Vivienne Westwood
open *SEX*, a boutique in
Chelsea's King's Road

● **1975** McLaren manages
notorious punk band the Sex
Pistols; they outrage polite
society, swear on TV, are the
polar opposite to chart-
hogging disco music—and
the kids love them

● **1977** The Sex Pistols' album
*Never Mind the Bollocks,
Here's the Sex Pistols* is
released and tops the
charts, not in spite but
because of its single "God
Save the Queen" being
banned by the BBC

BEGINNINGS

Critics **first used the term
"punk rock" in the early
1970s** to describe 1960s
garage bands. What **these
DIY musicians lacked in
formal training and cash**,
they made up for in rebellion.

FAMOUS PUNK BANDS:

- The Clash
- Buzzcocks
- Siouxsie and the Banshees
- Generation X
- Ramones
- The Damned
- The Cramps

**Punk spilled into fashion,
film, art, literature, and
all subdivisions of popular
culture.** Though other styles
of music have come along, for
many punk has never gone away.

NY CBGB

The Ramones, Blondie, Talking
Heads, and Johnny Thunder and the
Heartbreakers all played at CBGB,
establishing the New York style.

THE LONDON LOOK

**In the UK, political and economic
uncertainty had led to mass
unemployment.** London's youth
hung out at *SEX*, sometimes buying
clothes, more often improvising
their own with plastic bin bags,
bondage kits, safety pins, and a lot of
hairspray.

THE *CHALLENGER* DISASTER

On January 28, 1986, NASA's relatively routine space shuttle mission 51-L ended in tragedy.

 CHALLENGER A SPACE SHUTTLE, ONE OF THE WORLD'S FIRST REUSABLE SPACECRAFT

 MAIDEN VOYAGE APRIL 4, 1983

 LAUNCHED KENNEDY SPACE CENTER, CAPE CANAVERAL, FLORIDA, USA

 MISSION TO LAUNCH A NEW SATELLITE AND OPERATE ANOTHER SATELLITE OBSERVING HALLEY'S COMET

 PASSENGERS SEVEN ASTRONAUTS, INCLUDING TEACHER CHRISTINA MCAULIFFE, THE FIRST AMERICAN CIVILIAN IN SPACE

 SHUTTLE PROGRAM COST $200 BILLION (£155 BILLION)

PRELAUNCH PROBLEMS

The previous shuttle, *Columbia*, had been delayed landing, and extreme cold weather conditions had left **thick ice on the launch pad**.

WHAT HAPPENED?

Challenger's **external fuel tank collapsed, mixing fuel and propellant, causing them to ignite.** The shuttle orbiter broke away from the tank and broke up, but the section containing the crew continued to climb, before plummeting into the Atlantic Ocean.

WHAT KILLED THE CREW?

The crew were discovered still strapped into their seats. Although unclear, **it is probable they died from oxygen deficiency**. Ejector seats would not have saved them.

THE ROGERS COMMISSION

A team of experts, including astronaut **Neil Armstrong, test pilot Chuck Yeager, and physicist Richard Feynman**, were appointed to find the cause.

WHAT CAUSED THE FAILURE?

There were several contributing factors, including **a leak in the solid rocket booster joint**, which allowed superheated gas to escape, and **freezing temperatures** that meant two rubber O-rings failed to seal. **Fatal flaws in manufacturing, time-saving, and decision-making compounded the problems.**

AFTERMATH

NASA temporarily suspended manned flight until 1988, when it launched *Discovery*. A second disaster occurred on **February 1, 2003**, when **space shuttle Columbia disintegrated on reentry**, again killing all crew.

NUMBERS

9
Successful missions already flown by *Challenger*

11:39 A.M.
Liftoff

73 SECONDS
Time between liftoff and the disaster

46,000 FT.
Altitude at which the fireball occurred

40 FT.
Length of the tongue of flame emitted from the leak

200 MPH
Speed at which *Challenger* hit the Atlantic Ocean

THE CHERNOBYL NUCLEAR DISASTER

In 1986 workers preparing to conduct tests at the Chernobyl nuclear plant accidentally triggered the worst disaster in the history of nuclear power production.

 DATE APRIL 25–26, 1986

 LOCATION PRIPYAT IN PRESENT-DAY UKRAINE; 10 MILES FROM CHERNOBYL, 80 MILES FROM KIEV

 POPULATION BETWEEN 30,000 AND 50,000

 NUCLEAR POWER PLANT BUILT BY THE SOVIET UNION IN 1977, PRODUCING 1,000 MEGAWATTS OF ELECTRIC POWER

 DISASTER LOCATION REACTOR UNIT 4

WHAT HAPPENED?

Workers shut down the power regulation, emergency safety, and cooling systems, withdrawing most of the control rods from the core. **Xenon gas built up** and a chain reaction led to **a core meltdown and explosions that blew the reactor's lid**, releasing radioactive debris.

SECRECY

The Soviet government kept quiet about the incident, but **Swedish meteorologists noticed abnormal amounts of radioactivity in the atmosphere**, and officials were forced to admit the accident.

FIRST RESPONDERS

Helicopters dropped sand and boron onto the flames to quell the fires and prevent further nuclear reaction.

CLEAN-UP

Residents were not evacuated for thirty-six hours. In a highly dangerous process, **the plant** was shut down and **contained in a concrete sarcophagus**, but millions of acres of forest and farmland remained contaminated.

CONSEQUENCES

Thousands were eventually evacuated, though many more remained just outside the exclusion zone. **Livestock was born deformed and humans have since experienced radiation-induced illnesses and thyroid cancer.**

2
Chernobyl plant workers died the same night; **28** died in the immediate aftermath

 1,000 TONS
Weight of the steel cap blown away by the force

 8 DAYS
Length of time fires raged

 C.200
People directly exposed

 800
Sites where radioactive debris was buried

 18 MILES
Radius of the exclusion zone around the plant, covering about 1,000 square miles; it was later expanded to 1,600 square miles

 C.335,000
Number of people permanently relocated over several years

THE BERLIN WALL

A great barrier wall, surrounding the part of Berlin belonging to West Germany, prevented access between west and east Berlin for nearly thirty years.

 BUILT OVERNIGHT ON AUGUST 12–13, 1961 BY THE GERMAN DEMOCRATIC REPUBLIC (GDR/DDR)

 CONSTRUCTION BARBED WIRE AND CINDER BLOCKS, LATER CONCRETE

 HEIGHT 12 FT.

LENGTH 96 MILES, 27 MILES OF WHICH DIVIDED THE CITY

Guarded by **302 watchtowers, electrification, dogs, booby-trapped machine guns, floodlights, and mines**; soldiers shot escapees on sight.

WHY WAS IT BUILT?

After World War II, Germany was occupied by the four victorious Allies. **The eastern part was taken by the Soviet Union**, and Germany's former capital, **Berlin, was also split among the four**.

PURPOSE

The *Antifaschistischer Schutzwall* or "antifascist bulwark" was ostensibly **to prevent western "fascists" contaminating East Germany**. In reality it was to stop East Germans defecting.

CHECKPOINTS

Three checkpoints—Alpha, Bravo, and Charlie—screened officials traveling between the two Berlins. **There would eventually be twelve.**

THE FALL OF THE WALL

By 1989 the Soviet Union was beginning to disintegrate. In August fellow communist country Hungary opened its borders with Austria. People in East Germany began to demand similar freedom. The East German leader resigned.

The new government **decided to allow East Berliners to apply for visas to visit the West**, but the minister making the announcement was poorly briefed. Without first warning the border guards, he **said the changes were immediate**. Thousands of people gathered on both sides of the wall. **The guards could not hold them back and, on November 9, 1989, the border opened.**

2.5 MILLION
East Germans fled to the West 1949–61

C.5,000
East Germans escaped safely 1961–89

C.5,000
East Germans captured attempting to escape

171
killed trying to cross

NELSON MANDELA

Political activist, prisoner, South Africa's first black President – Nelson Mandela became one of the world's best-loved and most respected statesmen.

TIMELINE

July 18, 1918 Rolihlahla Mandela born in Mvezo, South Africa

1939 Enters Fort Hare, the only Western-style university for black people

1940 Sent home for taking part in a boycott

1944 Joins the ANC, becomes a key figure and establishes a youth league

1948 Apartheid is introduced

1949 The ANC begins a campaign of boycotts, strikes, and civil disobedience

1952 Mandela cofounds the first black law firm

1960 Police fire on a peaceful protest, killing sixty-nine; the Sharpeville Massacre sets off riots and the ANC is banned

APARTHEID

Hospitals, schools, bathrooms, and beaches were labeled "white" or "colored"; the facilities of the black majority were always worse than those of the white minority. Black people were not allowed to vote.

PRISON

Robben Island was a former leper colony. Mandela was given hard labor in a lime quarry. His cell had neither bed nor plumbing. The authorities forbade photos from the prison, or his being publicly quoted.

FREE NELSON MANDELA

The ANC's campaign rallied around Mandela. Abroad, sympathizers encouraged product boycotts, concerts, and even a song in his honor.

MADIBA

Mandela was often referred to by his Xhosa clan name as a mark of respect.

27
Years in jail

1961 Mandela cofounds Umkhonto we Sizwe (Spear of the Nation), the ANC's armed wing

1964 Mandela is imprisoned on Robben Island

1980 The "Free Nelson Mandela" campaign brings his story to the world

1990 Mandela is freed

1991 Apartheid is abolished

1993 Mandela is awarded the Nobel Peace Prize

1994 Elections held with votes for all; Mandela is pronounced President

1995 South Africa hosts the Rugby World Cup; Mandela's support for the mainly white team helps unite the country

December 5, 2013 Mandela dies in Johannesburg

THE TIANANMEN SQUARE MASSACRE

In 1989 peaceful protests by students calling for democracy were brutally put down by the Chinese Army.

 DATE JUNE 4, 1989

 LOCATION TIANANMEN SQUARE, BEIJING, CHINA

 COMBATANTS STUDENTS AND CITIZENS VS CHINA'S PEOPLE'S LIBERATION ARMY

 CASUALTIES UNKNOWN

THE PROTEST BEGINS

The **death in April of Hu Yaobang, prodemocratic official**, sparked a series of demonstrations that lasted several weeks and spread to other cities.

WESTERN INTEREST

A number of Western journalists, in town to cover the visit of Soviet leader Mikhail Gorbachev, started to report the story, causing anger and embarrassment to the Chinese government.

THE GODDESS OF DEMOCRACY

In the last two weeks of May, **martial law was imposed, but troops couldn't reach Tiananmen Square** due to the number of demonstrators. **Protesters focused around a plaster statue, the goddess of democracy.**

THE MASSACRE

- On the night of **June 3–4, tanks and heavily armed troops fired at will into the crowd**, shooting or mowing down anyone in their way.
- Thousands fled, but shootings continued throughout the day.
- **By June 5, rigid control had been regained** at the expense of hundreds, perhaps thousands of lives. **More protesters were later imprisoned or executed.**

TANK MAN

A famous photograph of **a single protestor facing a line of tanks** became synonymous with the atrocity. His identity—and fate—are still unknown.

TIANANMEN SQUARE IN NUMBERS

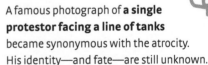

0

There are no reliable statistics available regarding any part of the incident.

Still a sensitive subject, public commemoration of the incident is banned in China, though annual vigils are held elsewhere.

THE DEATH OF THE PEOPLE'S PRINCESS

The mass outpouring of public grief following the death of Diana, Princess of Wales, was virtually unprecedented in stiff-upper-lipped Britain.

CAST

HRH PRINCE CHARLES Heir to the British throne
DIANA, PRINCESS OF WALES Prince Charles's divorced wife
DODI AL-FAYED Son of Harrods owner Mohamed Al-Fayed
HENRI PAUL Deputy head of security at the Ritz Hotel, Paris
TREVOR REES-JONES Diana's bodyguard
THE PAPARAZZI A pack of press photographers

Prince Charles and Diana were divorced in 1996. In 1997 **Diana began a relationship with Dodi Al-Fayed**, which became the subject of intense interest in the tabloid press, who sniffed marriage in the air. **On August 30, 1997, the couple arrived at the Ritz Hotel in Paris.**

TIMELINE

23:30 The couple leave the hotel and head for an apartment on the Champs-Élysées

00:25 Pursued by paparazzi on motorcycles, Henri Paul's speeding limousine crashes in a tunnel under the Pont de l'Alama; Paul and Dodi Al-Fayed are killed; Diana and Trevor Rees-Jones are seriously injured

04:00 Diana is declared dead; Rees-Jones survives

05:09 A short statement is issued by Buckingham Palace

11:00 UK Prime Minister Tony Blair describes Diana as **"the People's Princess"**

PUBLIC GRIEF

Reaction was immediate and visceral. **Within hours** Kensington Palace was **an ocean of flowers**.

BLAME GAME

Official blame rested with **Henri Paul, nearly three times over the drink-drive limit**. The public widely placed fault with **the paparazzi**.

FUNERAL

Billions of people around the world watched Diana's **lavish funeral on September 6**.

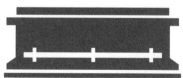

9/11

On September 11, 2001, four hijacked passenger planes were used as weapons on a suicide mission attacking the very heart of America. After 9/11, nothing would be the same again.

THE PLANES

 PLANE UA FLIGHT 11 BOEING 767 BOSTON TO LA, **92 PEOPLE ON BOARD**

 PLANE UA FLIGHT 77, BOEING 757 DULLES INT., WASHINGTON, DC TO LA, **64 PEOPLE ON BOARD**

 **PLANE UA FLIGHT 175, BOEING 767** BOSTON TO LA, **65 PEOPLE ON BOARD**

 PLANE UA FLIGHT 93, BOEING 757 NEWARK TO SAN FRANCISCO, **44 PEOPLE ON BOARD**

TIMELINE

(EASTERN STANDARD TIME)

8:19 a.m. Ground staff are alerted that Flight 11 has been hijacked; National Guard fighter planes are deployed

8:46 a.m. Mohammed Atta's hijackers crash Flight 11 into the North Tower of the World Trade Center

9:03 a.m. Flight 175 crashes into floors 75–85 of WTC's South Tower

9:37 a.m. Flight 77 crashes into the western side of the Pentagon

9:42 a.m. All U.S. flights are grounded

9:45 a.m. The White House and Capitol Building are evacuated

9:59 a.m. The South Tower of the WTC collapses

10:07 a.m. Learning about the attacks from friends, the passengers and crew of Flight 93 attack the hijackers, who crash the plane into a field in Pennsylvania

10:28 a.m. The WTC North Tower collapses

8:30 p.m. President Bush addresses the nation

WHAT HAPPENED?

Each of **the planes had been hijacked**. The authorities were alerted by cabin crew of the first attack, but before National Guard fighter planes could be deployed, **two had been flown into the World Trade Center**. Everyone on board each of the planes was killed; thousands of people on the ground also died.

AL QAEDA

The terrorist group, led by Osama bin Laden, believed the U.S. to be weak, and certainly it revealed weaknesses in America's national security, though these were quickly rectified.

THE TWIN TOWERS

After the collapse, "Ground Zero" became a place of pilgrimage. A memorial museum now stands there, including a single "survivor tree."

2,750
people killed in New York

184
killed at the Pentagon

40
killed in Pennsylvania

ALL 19 TERRORISTS DIED

400
police and firefighters killed

AFTERMATH

Millions watched in horror as TV replayed footage throughout the day. **For the first time in its history, NATO invoked Article 5**, which allowed members to respond collectively. On **October 7 the United States launched an attack against Afghanistan**, beginning a long and bloody war.

CHRONOLOGY

C.1420S–1670S European nations begin to explore beyond the known world

C.1330S–1350S The Black Death spreads across Europe, killing millions

C.1400S–1600S The Renaissance sees a flourishing of art and science

C.1300–1521 The Aztec Empire flourishes in South and Central America

C.1439 Johannes Gutenberg invents the printing press

1515 Martin Luther attacks the Catholic Church

1508–13 Nicolaus Copernicus outlines his theories of planetary motion

1478 The Spanish Inquisition starts to investigate the faith of converted Catholics

1526 The Mughal Empire is founded in northern India

1534 The Act of Supremacy declares Henry VIII Supreme Head of the Church of England

1620 The *Mayflower* sails for America, carrying Protestant separatists

1632 Construction begins on the Taj Mahal

1649 The Execution of Charles I shakes the concept of the divine right of kings

1660 The English monarchy is restored

1692 The Salem Witch Trials take place in America

1756 Wolfgang Amadeus Mozart is born

1776 Thirteen delegates sign the American Declaration of Independence

1783 The Treaty of Paris formally ends the American Revolution

1787 The First Fleet leaves Britain for Australia

1789 The French Revolution begins

1804 Napoleon Bonaparte crowns himself emperor

1811 South America begins the struggle for Independence

1825 The Stockton–Darlington Railway signals a transport revolution

1833 Slavery is abolished in the UK

1861 Civil War begins in America

1867 Karl Marx publishes *Das Kapital*

1868 The Boshin War signals the end of the Japanese shoguns

1897 The National Union of Women's Suffrage Societies is formed

1898 Chinese "Boxers" begin to attack foreigners, attracting fierce retaliation

1903 Orville Wright keeps an aircraft in the air for twelve seconds

1914 The assassination of Archduke Franz Ferdinand sparks World War I

1917 Revolution begins in Russia

1918 Spanish Flu kills tens of millions

1929 The U.S. Stock Market crashes, triggering the Great Depression

1936 The Spanish Civil War starts

1939 The Nazi invasion of Poland signals the beginning of World War II

1941 The Japanese attack on Pearl Harbor brings the U.S. into World War II

1945 Victory in Europe

1945 The world's first atomic bomb is dropped on Hiroshima

1947 India gains independence

1947 Ten Hollywood luminaries refuse to cooperate with the House Un-American Activities Committee

1949 Chairman Mao declares the People's Republic of China

1953 Revolution in Cuba brings communism close to the United States

1955 The Vietnam War begins

1955 Rosa Parks refuses to yield her bus seat, fueling the Civil Rights Movement

1960 The contraceptive pill is made available to American women

1962 The Cuban Missile Crisis brings the world perilously close to nuclear war

1969 *Apollo 11* puts the first man on the Moon

1989 Peaceful prodemocracy protests are brutally put down in Tiananmen Square

1990 Nelson Mandela is freed from jail

2001 Four hijacked planes devastate America in the 9/11 attacks

FURTHER READING

For centuries, historians, biographers, and philosophers have been trying to understand what made events happen when they did, the way they did. They have rarely come up with the same answers. Occasionally they don't even agree on dates. Some are impenetrably academic, others more accessible but delve less deeply. A book like this can only scratch at a very large surface.

General histories of the world are, by their very nature, general, but can be a good next step. *The New Penguin History of the World*, by J. M. Roberts, periodically revised, is widely regarded as a modern classic. For the traditionally minded, *Encyclopedia Britannica*, now online, includes entries about practically any aspect of life; history is a speciality.

Every subject dealt with here has had entire libraries of books written about it; to recommend just a few, calls for some tough decisions. Biographies of the early explorers, such as Laurence Bergreen's *Columbus: The Four Voyages* and *Over the Edge of the World: Magellan's Terrifying Circumnavigation of the Globe* seem a good place to begin.

John Bossy's *Christianity in the West 1400–1700* is a fine primer that guides the reader through many aspects of the Reformation. Antonia Fraser's *Six Wives of Henry VIII* explores the many human aspects of the split in the British church, state, and politics; her treatment of *Mary, Queen of Scots* is also highly recommended.

The Slave Trade: The Story of the Atlantic Slave Trade 1440–1870 by Hugh Thomas is an in-depth exploration of a difficult subject, while *Under the Black Flag* by David

Cordingly takes a long, hard look at the golden age of piracy. For books about the British in India, any of William Dalrymple's works are worth a read, especially *The Last Mughal*.

Gordon Wood's *The American Revolution* and Bernard Bailyn's *Ideological Origins of the American Revolution* are widely admired, while James McPherson's *Battle Cry of Freedom* lends insight into the American Civil War. For a highly readable, alternative impression of the Chicago World's Fair, try Eric Larson's *The Devil in the White City*.

Michael Howard's *The First World War* is an excellent introduction to World War I, while Michael Burleigh's *The Third Reich: A New History* provides background to Adolf Hitler and World War II. *The Cold War* by John Lewis Gaddis takes a closer look at the world after, while *Mao: The Unknown Story* is a disconcerting read by Jung Chang and Jon Halliday.

Tom Wolfe's exploration of the NASA space program, *The Right Stuff*, is superb, bettered only perhaps by astronaut Jim Lovell's highly readable account of the *Apollo 13* mission, *Lost Moon*. Nothing beats an account by someone who was actually there. *All the President's Men* by Carl Bernstein and Bob Woodward is the story of their own role uncovering the Watergate scandal. Nelson Mandela's autobiography *Long Walk to Freedom* became an instant bestseller. On the 9/11 terror attacks, history still has a long way to run, but Laurence Wright's *The Looming Tower: Al Qaeda's Road to 9/11* is an impressive account of what is known so far.

ENGLISH MONARCHS FROM 1066

Norman Kings
William I (The Conqueror) 1066–87
William II 1087–1100
Henry I 1100–1135
Stephen 1135–54

The Plantagenets
Henry II 1154–89
Richard I 1189–99
John 1199–1216
Henry III 1216–72
From here realm includes Wales
Edward I 1272–1307
Edward II 1307–27
Edward III 1327–77
Richard II 1377–99

House of Lancaster
Henry IV 1399–1413
Henry V 1413–22
Henry VI 1422–61

House of York
Edward IV 1461–83
Edward V 1483
Richard III 1483–85

The Tudors
Henry VII 1485–1509
From here the realm includes Ireland
Henry VIII 1509–47
Edward VI 1547–53
Mary I 1553–58
Elizabeth I 1558–1603

The Stuarts
From here the realm includes Scotland
James I (VI of Scotland) 1603–25
Charles I 1625–49

The Commonwealth
Oliver Cromwell, Lord Protector 1653–58
Richard Cromwell 1658–59

Restored Monarchy
Charles II 1660–85
James II (VII of Scotland) 1685–88
William III and Mary II 1680
Anne 1702–14

The Hanoverians
George I 1714–27
George II 1727–60
George III 1760–1820
George IV 1820–30
William IV 1830–37
Victoria 1837–1901

House of Saxe-Coburg and Gotha
Edward VII 1901–10

House of Windsor
George V 1910–36
Edward VIII 1936
George VI 1936–52
Elizabeth II 1952—

U.S. PRESIDENTS

George Washington 1789–97

John Adams 1797–1801

Thomas Jefferson 1801–09

James Madison 1809–17

James Monroe 1817–25

John Quincy Adams 1825–29

Andrew Jackson 1829–37

Martin Van Buren 1837–41

William Henry Harrison 1841

John Tyler 1841–45

James K. Polk 1845–49

Zachary Taylor 1849–50

Millard Fillmore 1850–53

Franklin Pierce 1853–57

James Buchanan 1857–61

Abraham Lincoln 1861–65

Andrew Johnson 1865–69

Ulysses S. Grant 1869–77

Rutherford Birchard Hayes 1877–81

James A. Garfield 1881

Chester A. Arthur 1881–85

Grover Cleveland 1885–89

Benjamin Harrison 1889–93

Grover Cleveland 1893–97

William McKinley 1897–1901

Theodore Roosevelt 1901–09

William H. Taft 1909–13

Woodrow Wilson 1913–21

Warren G. Harding 1921–23

Calvin Coolidge 1923–29

Herbert Hoover 1929–33

Franklin D. Roosevelt 1933–45

Harry S. Truman 1945–53

Dwight D. Eisenhower 1953–61

John F. Kennedy 1961–63

Lyndon B. Johnson 1963–69

Richard M. Nixon 1969–74

Gerald R. Ford 1974–77

Jimmy Carter 1977–81

Ronald Reagan 1981–89

George Bush 1989–93

Bill Clinton 1993–2001

George W. Bush 2001–09

Barack Obama 2009–17

Donald J. Trump 2017—